Swift during the Oxford Ministry

SWIFT

SWIFT

By
CARL VAN DOREN

LONDON
MARTIN SECKER
1931

LONDON: MARTIN SECKER LTD.
NUMBER FIVE JOHN STREET ADELPHI

CONTENTS

ILLUSTRATIONS

POOR RELATION

JONATHAN SWIFT aimed at mankind the most venomous arrow that scorn has ever yet let loose. Mankind, bland abstraction, caught his arrow, laughed at it, and turned it over to children to play with. Children, inoculated with *Gulliver's Travels* at an age when it cannot harm them, are thereafter innocently immune. If they hear of Swift they recollect their toy, unaware that it was intended to be deadly or that it has still lost little of its furious poison. Mankind, by a stroke so bold that it must have been indifferent, has protected itself. Swift remains a show, the story of his wild assault fades from the record. Touch the pages of the record, however, and it blazes, a story of fire in a language of ice.

Everywhere fire and ice, everywhere together. " Remember," Swift wrote to a woman who loved him as only men like Swift are loved, " that riches are nine parts in ten of all that is good in life." Though he was, when he said this, designing to chill a love which was warmer than he wanted it, design alone would not have been enough to prompt these cold words. He could not have formed them if they had not come from what he felt to be his reason and what he believed

9

to be his experience. Always he refused to speak about his fate except in the hard accents of reason. Always he refused to share in passions, outside his experience, which might have transformed the universe for him, softening it and comforting him. Even when they were offered, Swift held back, obstinate and doubtful. He could imagine no easier freedom. He could imagine no kinder world.

This caution, in a nature so imperious, had to be learned early to be learned at all. Swift learned it from an expert teacher waiting for him when he was born. Poverty of different degrees might have bred him to resignation or to unconcern, to holiness or to out-lawry. Swift's poverty had a subtler craft. It fed and clothed and housed everything about him but his pride. Had that been the mild vanity which is what most young men mean by pride, he might have gone through his dependent years unscarred. But the pride of Swift was constitutional, ceaseless, sensitive, and headlong. Nourished, it would still have fretted ; starved, it rebelled and gave itself to rage for want of action.

" And this it is," he wrote at twenty-five, " which a person of great honour in Ireland (and who was pleased to stoop so low as to look into my mind) used to tell me, that my mind was like a conjured spirit that would do mischief if I would not give it employment."

The conjured spirit often brooded over events older than its birth, telling itself that its mishaps had begun with its ancestors. To go no further back, there was Swift's grandfather, Thomas Swift, vicar of Goodrich in Herefordshire. He had been so stubborn and defiant a victim of Parliament during the Civil War that when he died in 1658 he had had no longer any fortune to be divided among his many sons and daughters. At least five of his sons had consequently taken to the law. All five of them had gone to Ireland, which was then poor enough to lack lawyers but not poor enough to be overlooked by Englishmen in search of a conquered province where they might have the benefit of their blood as well as of their merits.

Within six or seven years after the father's death Godwin, Dryden, Abraham (a merchant), William Jonathan, and Adam Swift had established themselves in Dublin. Godwin, four times married, had prospered most. He had had three heiresses in the steady series of his wives, and had made other advantageous speculations. Jonathan had prospered least. Trusting to a minor post as steward of the King's Inns, he had married the dowerless Abigail Erick of Leicestershire, begot a daughter, begot a son, and died. He left his widow a few debts, a few arrears due her if she could collect them, and an income of twenty pounds a year. When the posthumous son was born, 30th November, 1667, he became at once a general charge upon a family which was itself dispersed and insecure.

Dispersed and insecure, and yet too mindful of its rank to decline smoothly to a lower. Had not Barnam Swift, of the Yorkshire branch, been made an Irish viscount by Charles I, and had not his daughters married one of them the Earl of Eglinton and the other that Robert Feilding who for a third or fourth wife was to have, somewhat bigamously, a former mistress of Charles II ? Had not the wife of Thomas Swift, vicar of Goodrich, been the niece of Sir Erasmus Dryden ? Had not the wife of Thomas Swift, son of the vicar of Goodrich, been the daughter of Sir William Davenant ? Had not the first wife of Godwin Swift been a cousin of the Marchioness of Ormond ? Had not the Swifts as a rule, whether in Yorkshire or Kent or Herefordshire or Ireland, married like gentlemen ? Had they not lived as much like gentlemen as the shifting past century had permitted, holding on to land, gaining place by favour ? Was not Godwin Swift, head of the house in Ireland, attorney-general of the Palatinate of Tipperary because his first, though not his present, wife was related to the Ormonds who had favoured him ?

The Irish Swifts might be unsettled, but they went their ways in the shadow of distinction and the light of expectations. For one of them, the one genius of the race, there was in his youth no relief from the bitter contrast between his birthright and his circumstances. As a Swift he could not dig. As Jonathan Swift he could not beg. He had to accommodate himself to the moods of a family's charity.

How poor he was must be measured not by his needs but by his pride. His mother lived in Hoey's Court, then respectable enough. She had a nurse whose devotion to him appears in the only incident recorded of his early childhood. When he was a year old, Swift himself tells, this nurse, " who was a woman of Whitehaven, being under an absolute necessity of seeing one of her relations, who was then extremely sick, and from whom she expected a legacy, and being at the same time extremely fond of the infant, she stole him on shipboard unknown to his mother and uncle and carried him with her to Whitehaven, where he continued for almost three years. For when the matter was discovered his mother sent orders by all means not to hazard a second voyage till he could be better able to bear it. His nurse was so careful of him that before he returned he had learned to spell ; and by the time that he was three years old he could read any chapter in the Bible." This was no beggar's brat. And after the child's return to Dublin, whether he lived with his mother in Hoey's Court or at his uncle's house in Chancery Lane, there was little change in his condition. He was fed and clothed and housed.

But when at six he was sent to Kilkenny School there was a change. His mother had gone, or soon went, with her daughter to her own people in Leicester. The boy was more than ever dependent upon his uncle, who had chosen this school because it was under the patronage of the Ormonds. It is possible only to guess wherein Godwin Swift, who kept the boy in the school for the next eight years, fell short of what the nephew expected. Perhaps he stinted him in affection ; perhaps he stinted him in pocket-money. That the busy lawyer had not much tenderness to give to a random nephew, or that he had less money to distribute than his hungry clan supposed, is now easy to understand. It was not easy for a schoolboy to understand. This schoolboy, increasing in pride and exigence,

13

blamed his growing discontent upon his kinsman. Like other restive children, he cast himself as the tragic hero in an imagined drama of neglect, multiplying his adversities with an angry egotism.

" I remember, when I was a little boy," he wrote long afterwards, " I felt a great fish at the end of my line, which I drew up almost to the ground ; but it dropped in, and the disappointment vexes me to this very day, and I believe it was the type of all my future disappointments." He had formed his habits of brooding early, if he could be so deeply disappointed as never to forget this mischance, if he could regard the fish, flopping to preserve its life, as somehow in league against the tragic hero.

Nothing at Kilkenny broke up the drama of neglect in which he played his resentful part. Intellectually he was not precocious. He excelled among the young grammarians, if at all, only by his knack at dog-Latin and rhymed macaronics. His temper did not dispose him towards obedience to his masters or towards cheerfulness among his companions. He was on good terms with his cousin Thomas, son of the son of the vicar of Goodrich, sent over from England where his father died young, and with a boy named Francis Stratford, with whom Swift during his subsequent days of power in London often dined. With William Congreve, also English, also in Ireland because his father had sought a post there, Swift was later to be on kind if not close terms. But there is nothing to prove that in Congreve, two years younger than he, any more than in Thomas Swift or Stratford, Swift found at school a friend who met his demanding eagerness.

However far he may have gone in his conscious Ishmaelism at Kilkenny, he went farther at Trinity College, Dublin, to which, with his cousin Thomas and a few months after his friend Stratford, he was admitted as a pensioner in April 1682. There, in his own words, " by the ill-treatment of his nearest relations he was so discouraged and sunk in his spirits that he too much neglected his academic studies, for some parts of which he had no great relish by nature, and turned himself to reading history and poetry, so that when the time came for taking his degree of bachelor of arts, although he lived with great regularity and due observance of the statutes, he was stopped of his degree for dullness and insufficiency ; and at last hardly admitted in a manner, little to his credit, which is called in that college *spcciali gratia* on the 15th February, 1685 [1686] with four more on the same footing ; and this discreditable mark, as I am told, stands upon record in their college registry."

Plain words, but not altogether disinterested. Back of them appears the tragic hero's instinct to accuse the inimical or, at best, obtuse world in which he moved at Trinity. What the dispassionate records show is that the special grace by which he was admitted to the degree was an indulgence. A part of his work being unsatisfactory, he might have been required to wait another year. He was instead admitted on his general standing. No less than Thomas Swift, reported *mediocriter* in all three subjects of the examination preceding the degree, and no less than Stratford, *mediocriter* in one and *vix mediocriter* in two of them, Jonathan Swift, *male* in philosophy, *bene* in Greek and Latin, and *negligenter* in his Latin essay, became a bachelor of arts. Nothing but a little annoyance and a Latin phrase differentiated his wilful degree from their mediocre ones. Moreover, he remained at Trinity three years longer, and would have become a master of arts there if the Revolution had not driven him elsewhere early in 1689.

Swift had seemed insufficient only because he was impatient. Contemptuous of philosophy, which he thought " vain babbling, and a mere sound of words," and careless of Latin prose, by which he planned to live no more than by philosophy, he would not give to them the slight attention which would have been enough. He would read only on his own impulse, for his own purpose, and without pedantry. " If a rational man reads an excellent author with just application he shall find himself extremely improved, and perhaps insensibly led to imitate that author's perfections, although in a little time he should not remember one word in the book, nor even the subject it handled ; for books give the same turn to our thoughts and way of reasoning that good and ill company do to our behaviour and conversation ; without either loading our memories or making us even sensible of the change."

Swift's reading was always an experience. In a world too narrow for his powers he turned to poets and historians, who, he discovered and later said, enlarge the mind and thoughts, extend and refine the imagination, direct the judgment, lessen the " admiration," and increase the fortitude of their readers. For such experiences, during his seven years at college, the academic penalty of being called irregular was not a ruinous price.

For Swift, however, too proud to be bored and yet too proud to go without the rewards of boredom, it was humiliation. He was a rebel who could not quite glory in his rebellion. If, perversely, he flung himself now and then into irregularities of conduct, they left him unsatisfied. Nor were they, it appears, important. He was fined for absences from chapel and from lectures ; he was fined for " town-haunting," which meant not being present at nine each evening when the roll of students was called over. On the date of his twenty-first birthday, a few weeks before he left the college, a " Sir Swift," either Jonathan or Thomas, was censured for being contumacious and contemptuous to the junior dean, suspended for a month, and ordered to beg pardon, on his knees and publicly, to the insulted officer. This was of course nearly three years after Jonathan's degree, and may indicate that he had fallen off from his regularity and observance of the statutes. He had now passed seven years in Dublin. The town had possibly come to tempt him as much as the college bored him. His later days at the University, however, were devoted rather to idleness and scorn than to the ordinary vices of young men.

Drunkenness, gambling, lechery, and rioting were as uncongenial to him as scholastic disputation. These were for looser minds than his. He had the pride of intellect which fosters virtue by making vice seem trifling by comparison, the vagary of feeble wills, the waste of energy diverted. He could not help realizing that irregularity was folly, and that it was absurd for him to have lost what fools had won by merely being regular. His instincts were profoundly on the side of order. When he disobeyed it was only because he was denied the opportunity to command.

As tragic hero in his own drama he blamed his faults upon the ill-treatment of his relations, chiefly his uncle Godwin. The accusation is melodrama. Godwin Swift so declined from his prosperity during these same years that his health gave way, his mind failed, and he died soon after, leaving a broken estate to his heirs. During the last stage he may well have had little money for his nephew, and less tact than ever in bestowing it, but his failure and death were hardly spite. Towards William Swift, " the best of my relations," to whom the nephew thereafter owed his principal support, and towards certain other uncles and cousins, Swift felt gratitude. It was Godwin whom he accused of giving him the education of a dog. The nephew was as unjust as the uncle was untactful.

All that Swift needed to make him happy was a cheerful way of taking what he could get. All that he needed to make him blond was fair hair instead of black on his proud head and in the thick eyebrows under which his blue eyes burned and challenged out of a face in which discontent was being written over confidence.

These different needs were equally beyond his

18

reach. He could not be cheerful, because he was filled and driven by the sense and need of power. It was his heritage, richer than any he longed for. But it brought torment as well as exultation. He could not measure his endowment by that of his friends. They did the same things he did, and did them more successfully. He could not consult his elders. They would probably regard his sense of superiority as another half-grown delusion. He could not even have a full assurance of it himself, for it was dark and spasmodic, and it furnished no arguments to convince him that it was genuine. It was not yet conscious of half its aims. It stirred about in him without directing him where to go or what to undertake. It demanded knowledge, but not the information which it was his duty to acquire. It demanded eminence, but not any of the kinds of eminence to which he had access in school or college. It demanded expression, but in some powerful language which he had not yet learned. Above all, it demanded sway, over men and events. And Swift was poor, obscure, without influence, unable to endure his present fortunes, unable to decide what career would mend them.

Waiting bred impatience. Impatience set up friction. Friction hurt. He paid it back with an instinctive hatred which did not always trouble to be just to its objects. The fish at Kilkenny had disappointed him by living. His uncle in Dublin had disappointed him by dying. The world was full of disappointments, and he was the chosen victim.

Yet Swift's plight was not entirely melodrama which

he had elaborated to console himself. Telling Vanessa that riches are nine parts in ten of all that is good in life, he added : " and health is the tenth." On the whole, he suffered more from lack of health than from lack of money. Soon after he came of age he began to be afflicted with the " giddiness and coldness of the stomach " which he attributed to a surfeit of apples, and not long afterwards with the deafness which he attributed to catching cold by sitting on the ground. The causes which he fixed upon may not have been the real ones. The effects were real, and they harried and frightened him.

His malady, it now seems, was a form of auditory vertigo, the result perhaps of hæmorrhage in the labyrinth of the ear. In this, if he had known the truth, he might have found a stroke of malice more sly and vindictive than any which he thought to accuse his fate of. A little, invisible, incurable defect doomed him. While his pride towered and his wrath hurled its freezing accusations, fate could be patient, knowing that a physical disorder, petty in itself, had helped to rouse this spiritual tumult. At its own time it would quiet him more horribly than the most offended thunderbolt.

At twenty-one Swift, born to act incessantly, had not yet played a part in any actions except those which went on inside his own mind. Straitened in school and college, he had nevertheless been safe. The Revolution, which shook the hold of the English colonists, drove him hurriedly from Ireland to a passing refuge with his mother in Leicester. He never thought of him-

Swift as a Student at Trinity College

self as Irish, and always resented it if others thought him so. Though he had been born in Ireland, he had been a member of the English gentry planted there to rule it. He left because the aborigines, " the savage old Irish " he called them, had risen to overwhelm their conquerors. He was only returning to his true country, to make his fortune among his true compatriots. The Revolution hurried him, but his restless nature would in any case have impelled him, sooner or later, in the direction of a larger world than Ireland.

II

DEPENDENT

I

SWIFT'S prospects when he arrived at Leicester were not encouraging. He could hope for little from Ireland, and his mother lived on twenty pounds a year. She might be "of an easy, contented spirit," rising early and devoting her pious days to needle and book. Her son was of another temper. He chafed in the unexciting town, where he thought the inhabitants "a parcel of very wretched fools," given to lying and gossiping "above all parts that I was ever in." His energy would not let him rest. If he busied himself at all it was with the pastime most likely to engage a young man during restless leisure.

He philandered with Betty Jones, a cousin of his mother's. He philandered with other girls, then or at later visits, not so much out of interest in them as out of his need to exercise his powers upon whoever came within range of them. "It is this humour which makes me so busy when I am in company, to turn all that way ; and since it commonly ends in talk, whether it be love or common conversation, it is all alike. This is so common that I could remember twenty women in my life "—he was writing early in 1692—"to whom I behaved myself just the same way ; and I profess without any other design than that of entertaining myself when I am very idle, or when something goes amiss in my affairs."

To divert himself or to ease his frustration : these were the instincts which had already begun to involve Swift with women. His ruling instinct was towards action among stubborn men. In relaxed intervals he found it soothing to let his powers play over natures which seemed yielding and responsive. In frustrate intervals he turned greedily, even cruelly, to the same sport, to assure himself that he still had the faculty of dominion.

His flirtation with Betty Jones, troubling to his mother, came to an end, and the girl married an innkeeper. Swift before the close of 1689 joined the household of Sir William Temple as something less than secretary for twenty pounds a year. This connection again he owed to his uncles, who had been associated in Ireland with Temple's father and with Temple himself. " His whole family having been long known to me," Temple explained, " obliged me . . . to take care of him."

Swift went to Temple hoping to learn the ways of the world from a man, also from Ireland, who had risen to influence and very near to power. For Temple Ireland had been but a springboard. His career had led him to more impressive quarters of Europe. Having turned to England shortly after the Restoration, he had made friends at Court, had been sent to the Continent to safeguard British interests, and had

23

twice been ambassador at the Hague, where he had helped to bring about the hopeful marriage of William of Orange to the niece of the English king. Charles II, valuing his ambassador's astuteness and dexterity, had more than once offered to make him Secretary of State. He had each time refused, perceiving that Charles and his ministers had little use for other qualities which Temple valued in himself, and had taken to a serene retirement. Not even the accession of William and Mary, or their grateful offer of the post which he had refused at the hand of Charles, had been able to bring him back. He preferred to live at Moor Park, near Farnham, in Surrey, remembering the large actions in which he had taken part, and being a philosopher among the gardens, in the Dutch manner, which reminded him of the country where he had had his triumphs.

Swift found Temple a man looking at the world as in a mirror. No actual affairs now concerned him so much as those of his own past, of which he was writing his memoirs. Reminiscence had not made his judgment less firm and level than it had been while it was constantly being tested by the intrigues of disingenuous, unscrupulous men. He was enlightened, responsible, benevolent. But, never having been ambitious, he had remained an amateur. " When I was young and in some idle company, it was proposed that everyone should tell what their wishes should be, if they were sure to be granted ; some were very pleasant, and some very extravagant ; mine were health and peace and fair weather." Such desires had allowed Temple to cherish as a virtue what included a touch of weakness and vanity. His retirement had been, in part, surrender. Disgusted by the conduct of men less virtuous than he, but also weak and vain, he had retreated to a happy vacuum where he had gone on cherishing his virtue till it now glowed with the colours of a philosophic heroism.

Swift, a conjured spirit aching for employment, was employed as Temple's amanuensis while the master composed mellifluous essays on gardens, on health and long life, on popular discontents, on poetry, and on heroic virtue. Swift, starving for the world, might sometimes be allowed to keep pace with Temple when, leaving off his moral considerations, he walked in his gardens, along his trim canal, perhaps despising the new sciences which had lately come to the notice of gentlemen, and perhaps wondering from what herbs he could concoct more potent doses for his household and even for his hopeless, hereditary gout.

Between Swift and Temple there was enough difference to make a war, but there was no war. Neither of them entirely realized that they were wrong pupil and wrong teacher. Temple never realized it. Though he was kind enough, he was not, as he could not have been, enough concerned to see deeply into the vexed spirit forced to bend itself to his placid will. Recommending his dependent to Sir Robert Southwell in May 1690, he said of Swift only that " he has lived in my house, read to me, writ for me, and kept all accounts so far as my small occasions required. He has Latin and Greek, some French, writes a good and current hand, is very honest and diligent, and has good friends, though they have for the present lost their fortunes in Ireland." Any later conflicts between them Temple overlooked or forgave with calm magnanimity. At his death, after a decade of this service of talent by genius, " that great man," as Swift precisely put it, " beside a legacy left him the care and trust and advantage of publishing his posthumous writings." And on that same occasion the greater man wrote in his journal that with Temple had died " all that was good and amiable among men."

Swift may have been often bored by Temple's heroic virtue and by his amateur erudition. He may have felt bewildered when Temple " would look cold and out of humour for three or four days, and I used to suspect a hundred reasons." But the dependent judged his patron rather by his actions than by his poses. He had gone to Temple to better fortunes which were desperately low. He had lived nearer to the world than if he had become a fellow of Trinity. He had learned everything Temple had to teach.

What fretted Swift at Moor Park was not so much the character of his patron, or even the mere fact of his own dependence, as the unsatisfying uses to which he had to put his still undetermined powers. With all his pride, he could only serve, never command. With all his acuteness, he could not name his own gifts even to himself. When, after his first brief stay with Temple, he went to Ireland with a recommendation to Southwell in the summer of 1690, he could still consider a fellowship in the college which he hated. Failing to obtain that, or the degree which he had missed, he continued in Ireland for another restless year, further broken by ill-health, returned to his mother, and visited his cousin Thomas, who was now at Oxford reading for his degree at Balliol. Jonathan Swift, again at Moor Park by Christmas, may already have decided to turn from Trinity to Oxford, but it was the only decision he had reached before he settled back into his lowering dependence.

He helped his patron with other of his dilettante labours and copied the translations from Spanish poetry with which Lady Giffard, Temple's sister, embellished the leisure which she could spare from being Temple's chief of staff.

Between Lady Giffard and Swift there was, at least in time, a sharp hostility. If he was bored by the brother he was angered by the sister, whose record of long devotion was not enough to reconcile him to her present influence in the household. She, virtual chatelaine by reason of Lady Temple's illness, resented the secretary's unconcern. Lady Temple— " Mild Dorothea, peaceful, wise, and great "—Swift apparently liked. There was little to bring them into opposition. Nor was there manifest opposition between him and the other members of the family or the numerous dependents who had drifted to this patriarchal shelter. Among them all, however, he found no equal, no congenial friend. Urged by his pride to passions if not to frenzies, he could pour himself out neither in activity nor in confidences. Whatever refuge he had from his idleness and his secrecy was in the society of a child.

The child was Esther Johnson, whom Swift eventually called Stella. Her father, younger son of a good family in Nottinghamshire, had probably been a dependent of Temple who served as steward. But by 1689 he was dead, and his widow was companion to Lady Giffard. Bridget Johnson and her daughter, or daughters, lived at the edge of the Park in a cottage where Swift, after he had made friends there, could sometimes forget his subordination. Stella was eight years old when the young man, then twenty-two, arrived from Leicester. " Her hair was blacker than a raven, and every feature of her face in perfection," he said. " I . . . had some share in her education, by directing what books she should read, and perpetually instructing her in the principles of honour and virtue." He taught her to write, taught her so well that her handwriting could later be mistaken for his own. He taught himself to depend upon comforts which only she could give him during those restive years : admiration without analysis, affection without exigence, a child's obedience, a child's worship.

2

But Stella was for the present at most only an episode, a casual breathing-spell between battles. Not that Swift was overworked by Temple. He had too much time on his hands. " There is something in me which must be employed," he wrote in February of this second winter at Moor Park, " and when I am alone turns all, for want of practice, into speculation and thought ; insomuch that in these seven weeks I have been here, I have writ, and burnt and writ again, upon almost all manner of subjects, more perhaps than any man in England." What he wrote could hardly have been history. He had enough of that with Temple. It was not philosophy. Writing to his cousin Thomas in May he said he was getting up his Greek and Latin for the Oxford degree, " but to enter upon the causes of philosophy is what I protest I will rather die in a ditch than go about." It was probably poetry. Some of his poetry has survived.

That his poetry was bad means less than that it was Pindaric. For that Temple shares the blame. He advised Swift to write like Cowley, and Swift for a year or so fiercely beat imagined wings to raise himself to an alien elevation. Flight was not in him.

" It makes me mad," he wrote to his cousin, " to hear you talk of making . . . next morning . . . what I could not do under two or three days, nor does it enter into my head to make anything of a sudden but what I find to be exceeding silly stuff except by great chance. I esteem the time of studying poetry to be two hours in the morning, and that only when the humour sits, which I esteem for the flower of the whole day, and truly I make bold to employ them that way, and yet I seldom write above two stanzas in a week—I mean such as are to any Pindaric ode—and yet I have known myself in so good a humour as to make two in a day, but it may be no more in a week after, and when all is done I alter them a hundred times, and yet I do not believe myself to be a laborious dry writer, because if the fit comes not immediately I never heed it, but think of something else."

About this bad poetry he wrote bad prose, but the straggling clauses make clear what he did not know he said. Lacking the nature for poetry, he lacked the full desire; lacking the full desire, he lacked both the ease with which some true poets write and the passion which keeps the others from caring whether they write with ease or not. Swift was writing because he was raging. He wanted to be heard if he could not be felt. Poetry was a kind of power.

Being Swift, he could not take his struggles lightly. " I am over-fond of my own writings," he confided. " I would not have the world think so, for a million, but it is so, and I find when I write what pleases me I am Cowley to myself and can read it a hundred times over. I know it is a desperate weakness, and has nothing to defend it but its secrecy, and I know further that I am wholly in the wrong, but have the same pretence the baboon had to praise her children." The image is pleasant but incomplete. Though he might then set the baboon's value on his strophes, and might all his life hate his cousin John Dryden for telling him the truth about them, Swift within another year or so had come to hate them, with that hate which was twin to his love. Or rather, he had come to hate whatever it was that had fascinated and then disappointed him.

When he found his hope falling off with his delusion,

Swift turned furious and accusatory. In the last of his early poems he angrily renounced his Muse :

> " *Malignant Goddess ! bane to my repose,*
> *Thou universal cause of all my woes ;*
> *Say whence it comes that thou art grown of late*
> *A poor amusement of my scorn and hate. . . .*
> *To thee I owe that fatal bent of mind,*
> *Still to unhappy restless thoughts inclined ;*
> *To thee, what oft I vainly strive to hide,*
> *That scorn of fools, by fools mistook for pride. . . .*
> *Madness like this no fancy ever seized,*
> *Still to be cheated, never to be pleased.*
>   *. . . From this hour*
> *I here renounce thy visionary power ;*
> *And since thy essence on my breath depends,*
> *Thus with a breath the whole delusion ends.*"

Poetry had failed him. As soon as he had learned to be honest he said a bitter farewell. Then he went on to prose.

The second stay with Temple was not continually midnight. In July 1692, after a brief residence at Oxford, Swift received from Hart Hall, now Hertford College, the degree of master of arts. " I never was more satisfied," he wrote his uncle, " than in the behaviour of the University of Oxford to me. I had all the civilities I could wish for, and so many favours that I am ashamed to have been more obliged in a few weeks to strangers than ever I was in seven years to Dublin College." At Moor Park, too, his rank became more gratifying. Temple not only treated his secretary with confidence at home, among his memoirs and his gardens, but even trusted him abroad.

Once in the spring of 1693, when King William had sent the Earl of Portland to consult Temple about a proposed bill for triennial parliaments, Temple, who did not feel sure the Earl would carry his full message, sent Swift after him to Kensington. There the secretary talked with both Portland and the King. " But," as Swift himself related it, " all in vain. For the King by ill advisers was prevailed upon to refuse passing the bill. This was the first time that Mr. Swift had ever any converse with courts, and he told his friends it was the first incident that helped to cure him of vanity." But not, plainly, of pride, which had made him expect that his country counsel would naturally be taken.

These successes, however were too small to quiet his fierce restlessness, which with the decline of his Pindaric hopes began to clarify itself into satiric hatred. Just before he said his farewell to poetry he wrote some complimentary verses to Congreve, who had risen to a sudden fame in London with his first comedy. The compliments were confused. The lines in which Swift spoke of his own slow fortunes and his savage plans were as unmistakable as lightning. His " old unvanquish'd pride," he wrote, looked with scorn on half mankind, which must beware of impending maledictions. He wondered that the world could be so clumsy in the face of

" *My hate, whose lash just Heaven has long decreed*
Shall on a day make sin and folly bleed."

Did the world not know that his wrath was its ruin ?
This was language above the capacity of a dis-

appointed minor poet. It was fury, not peevishness, that lay behind Swift's threat. His fury, so long wasted in aimless blows at phantoms, had become confident. Such confidence, in a man who was not a fool, was a sign of dangerous powers gathering to attack. They might be in their present mood because they had so long been checked in their impulses towards action. They may have sullenly decided upon words because they saw no opportunity for deeds. But all their hatred was not the consequence of frustration. Hatred was native to Swift, as love was to St. Francis. If Swift has been more frequently misunderstood than St. Francis, it is because men are allowed to love without giving reasons for it, but not to hate.

The growth of Swift's purpose was of course not obvious to him, and it was not regular. No doubt he was often at peace in his occupations at Moor Park or in his relaxed intervals with Stella. His anger rose or fell with contrary or prosperous days. He could, like many men, be busy whether he was happy or unhappy. But by nature he was always restless. His energy drove him to violent exercise, particularly to walking, which he thought his health required. He liked to walk from Farnham to London, nearly forty miles away, and even to Leicester, stopping at dubious inns and amusing himself with the speech and customs of the people. Nor would his restlessness permit him to regard his dependence, outwardly comfortable, as more than a starting-point. His temper demanded independence.

With the help of his uncles he might possibly have become a lawyer. With the help of the King it is said that he might have become a captain of dragoons. With the help of Temple he might have become a clerk in the Rolls office at Dublin, and he was indeed offered such a post. But none of these careers suited his tastes or promised what he was looking for. Instead, he decided to take Orders and enter the Church. When Temple had failed to obtain for him, through the favour of the King, a prebend of Westminster or Canterbury, Swift chose to take his own steps.

He went to Ireland in May 1694, leaving Temple angry. But as soon as Swift humbly applied, in October of that year, for a certificate of " morals and learning " which would satisfy the Irish bishops that he had properly conducted himself since he left Trinity, Temple, relenting, furnished it. Swift was ordained deacon the same month and priest in the following January. Almost immediately he was appointed to the prebend of Kilroot, a rural parish near Belfast.

Though Swift had had scruples about entering the Church solely as a livelihood, there was no mystery in his position. " I look upon myself, in the capacity of clergyman," he said, " to be one appointed by Providence for defending a post assigned to me, and for gaining over as many enemies as I can. Although I think my cause is just, yet one great motive is my submitting to the pleasure of Providence, and to the laws of my country." As to belief : " To say a man is bound to believe is neither truth nor sense " ; " I am in all opinions to believe according to my own impartial reason ; which I am bound to inform and improve, as far as my capacity and opportunities will permit."

Yet Swift had no urge towards any heresy. " Violent zeal for truth," he thought, " hath an hundred to one odds to be either petulancy, ambition, or pride." Order was more important than zeal. " Liberty of conscience, properly speaking, is no more than the liberty of possessing our own thoughts and opinions, which every man enjoys without fear of the magistrate : but how far he shall publicly act in pursuance of those opinions is to be regulated by the laws of the country." " Every man, as a member of the commonwealth, ought to be content with the possession of his own opinion in private, without perplexing his neighbour or disturbing the public." So a soldier might reason, or a magistrate, or a prime minister. Swift was not a philosopher full of ideas, not a prospector for truths still to be found. Although, in spite of this rational attitude towards his calling, he later became jealously devoted to the Church, that was because they were his calling and his Church.

If he had any illusions as to what it might mean to rule in a parish, he lost them. Kilroot was dreary and remote, and Swift was no more contented in his uncomfortable independence than he was rich on his hundred pounds a year. One such year was as much as he could stand. He surrendered his prebend to a fellow-clergyman whom he had known at Oxford, and was back again at Moor Park two years after he had left it.

How idle and frustrate he had been appears from a letter he wrote just before his willing departure. The letter was to Jane Waring of Belfast, a cousin to two

35

men who had been students at Trinity when Swift was
there. With her, by Swift poetically called Varina, he
had carried on another of his flirtations. He had even
been involved to the point of a proposal. Cured of
poetry, he had not yet been cured of philandering. He
could still use, in writing to her, a language which
comes strangely from a pen assigned to the cause of
wrath.

"Impatience," he began, speaking of himself, " is
the most inseparable quality of a lover," and he explained, what none knew better than he, that " every
one who hunts after pleasure or fame or fortune is still
restless and uneasy till he has hunted down his game ;
and all this is not only very natural but something
reasonable too, for a violent desire is little better than
a distemper, and therefore men are not to blame in
looking after a cure."

When he began to speak of Varina he once more
flapped almost Pindaric wings. " That dearest object
upon which all my prospect of happiness entirely
depends is in perpetual danger to be removed for ever
from my sight. Varina's life is daily wasting . . . yet
some power that repines at human felicity has that
influence to hold her continually doating on her
cruelty, and me upon the cause of it. . . . Why was I
so foolish to put my hopes and fears into the power or
management of another ? " Having, however, subdued
his independence to his longing for her, he was eager
to forego all other prospects. For her he would stay in
Ireland, even in Kilroot. " But listen to what I here
solemnly protest, by all that can be witness to an oath,

that if I leave this kingdom before you are mine, I will endure the utmost indignities of fortune rather than ever return again, though the King would send me back his deputy."

In the midst of his passion Swift still seemed to be counting on a refusal, not, possibly, without a bearable sense of safety no matter how he might forecast his despair. "It was your pity opened the first way to my misfortune ; and now your love is finishing my ruin. And is it so then ? In one fortnight I must take eternal farewell of Varina, and I wonder will she weep at parting a little to justify her poor pretences of affection to me ? " The certainty of this eternal farewell made Swift free to bring up his reproaches. "The only felicity permitted to human life we clog with tedious circumstances and barbarous formality. By Heaven, Varina, you are more experienced, and have less virgin innocence than I. Would not your conduct make one think you were hugely skilled in all the little politic methods of intrigue ? "

Swift himself had been, he said, completely without craft, as without limits. Such a passion as his had " a property peculiar to itself, to be most commendable in its extremes." It was no more capable than piety of any blameworthy excess. Now he would withhold from her the full reality of his anguish. " O Varina, how imagination leads me beyond myself and all my sorrows ! It is sunk, and a thousand graves lie open ! No, Madam, I will give you no more of my unhappy temper, though I derive it all from you. . . . Only remember, that if you still refuse to be mine, you will quickly lose, for ever lose, him that is resolved to die as he has lived, all yours."

Protest as he might, Swift was in this letter surely as crafty as he was mawkish. He contrived to put Varina in the wrong so that she might seem to blame for the end of their provincial interlude. He had been playing at love because he had had nothing to work at. Now that he had something better to do, no doubt he meant to do it. But he preferred to take his leave with his broken heart in his hand. He could at once pay a generous tribute to the lady's charms and call attention to his own sad, proud, faithful carriage at the moment of defeat. His farewell, however, was not that of a lover who would grieve long. And Swift, soon back with Temple, quickly found exercise for his powers in concerns much nearer his heart than any possible Varina.

3

There was now little in his situation at Moor Park to fret his pride. He knew that if at any time his post became tedious or humiliating he could again turn for independence, at least, to the Church. He was a clergyman on leave, as he might have been a soldier temporarily out of active service. He was a man of learning, already entered upon a profession, who had consented to be of use to Temple in tasks which interested them both. Lady Temple had died. Temple, lonely, infirm, depended probably as much upon Swift's youth and strength as Swift upon Temple's wealth and influence.

Moreover, Stella, fifteen when Swift returned from Kilroot, was an old comfort and a new delight. "She was sickly from her childhood until about the age of fifteen ; but then grew into perfect health, and was looked upon as one of the most beautiful, graceful, and agreeable young women in London "—and here Swift, writing on the night of Stella's death, added his touch of ice—" only a little too fat." But at fifteen she could hardly yet have outgrown her design, or have come to stir in him the affection which he later felt. To her, or to her mother in the knowledge that it would reach Stella's eyes, he wrote cheerfully during one of their visits to London with Temple and Lady Giffard : " I desire your absence heartily, for now I live in great state, and the cook comes in to know what I please to have for dinner. I ask very gravely what is in the house, and accordingly give orders for a dish of pigeons. . . . You shall have no more ale unless you send us a letter. Here is a great bundle and a letter for you ; both came together from London. We all keep home like so many cats."

That Swift at thirty was at last learning to be easy in his letters is a sign, possibly, that he was happier, certainly that he was busier. " I myself was never miserable while my thoughts were in a ferment, for I imagine a dead calm is the troublesomest part of our voyage through the world." His calling chosen, Swift could read and write without the sense, like eating without hunger, that beyond his pleasure lay no purpose. Reading, he now knew better what to look for. Writing, he now knew better what to aim at.

39

For if reading to Swift was experience, writing was action. He later declared to Pope that "all my endeavours from a boy to distinguish myself were only for want of a great title and fortune, that I might be used like a lord by those who have an opinion of my parts : whether right or wrong it is no great matter ; and so the reputation of wit or great learning does the office of a blue ribbon or of a coach and six horses." He wrote to gain influence and to exert it. For literary reputation he cared almost as little as some gentlemen of letters say they care. He never took money for his writings except what " Mr. Pope's prudent management " got him for *Gulliver*. Swift might be fated by his gifts to captivate men's tastes and entertain their imaginations, but he wanted to master their wills and direct their conduct.

As a preacher he set himself to tell his congregations so clearly what their duty was that they could have no doubt and no excuse. As a journalist he used all his skill to move public opinion to political action. And by his satires he intended to clear the paths of mankind of the affectations, follies, and vices which tangled what he thought the straight course of virtue and order. For Swift the words he used were as bayonets to a soldier, verdicts to a magistrate, laws to a minister. When at thirty he turned to words in his campaign against fortune, he meant them to be more than words.

The character of his first satires was determined by his circumstances. Living a little out of the world, in Temple's walled, heroic realm, he had come to despise the buzzing wits and upstart scientists who, he thought, infested the moral and intellectual life of the times. Though Dryden was one of the wits and Newton one of the scientists, Swift did not bother to distinguish among them. His hatred was no more disposed to scrupulous justice than another man's love.

As Swift's cause was partly unjust, so was his ground for this attack partly accidental. Temple, stalking in virtue, had taken sides in the controversy, then disturbing France, over the relative merits of the ancients and the moderns. He had pronounced like a gentleman for the ancients. " I know of no new philosophers," Temple said, " that have made entries upon that noble stage for fifteen hundred years past, unless Descartes and Hobbes should pretend to it. . . . There is nothing new in astronomy to vie with the ancients, unless it be the Copernican system ; nor in physic, unless Harvey's circulation of the blood. . . . 'Tis agreed by the learned that the science of music so admired by the ancients is wholly lost in the world. . . . So as those two divine excellencies of music and poetry are grown, in a manner, but the one fiddling and the other rhyming. . . . What traces have we left of that admirable science or skill in architecture, by which such stupendous fabrics have been raised of old . . . that they hardly fall within our imagination ? . . . The arts of painting and statuary began to revive with learning in Europe, and made a great but short flight ; so as, for these last hundred years, we have not had one master, in either of them, who deserved a rank with those that flourished in that short period."

Temple could not know that Bach was then alive.

41

Having refused the embassy to Spain, he had missed a possible chance to hear about Velasquez. But he might, except for his rank and preoccupations, have met Rembrandt in Holland or Molière in France or Milton in England. He had not. He could with a peaceful conscience, plausibly, courteously, and only now and then ironically, dismiss the moderns.

Perhaps the chief fault of modern learning, he concluded, was that so many of the learned were not quite men of the world. " The shallow, the superficial, and the sufficient among scholars " had attracted ridicule, " and very justly, by pretending to more than they had, or to more esteem than what they had could deserve, by broaching it in all places, at all times, upon all occasions, and by living so much among themselves, or in their closets and cells, as to make them unfit for all other business and ridiculous in all other conversations." From this it had come about that true learning was confused with pedantry and that both suffered from the present mode of ridicule. " 'Tis the itch of our age and climate, and has overrun both the Court and the stage ; enters a House of Lords and Commons as boldly as a coffee house, debates of Council as well as private conversation ; and I have known in my life more than one or two ministers of state that would rather have said a witty thing than done a wise one ; and made the company laugh rather than the kingdom rejoice."

This was Temple's attitude, but so was it Swift's. Though the *Battle of the Books* and the *Tale of a Tub* may have been planned at Kilroot and subsequently revised in London, they were the fruits, however unexpected, of that suave garden at Moor Park. Swift took the superiority of the ancients for granted, with nothing but ridicule for any modern who doubted it. The contemporary world of learning he assumed to be made up almost altogether of mean, starved, envious, strident, stingless fools and fops, ignorant and arrogant, who swarmed about their betters with a fly's equal appetite for dung or honey.

Where Swift differed from Temple was where genius differs from talent, not in mere attitude but in art and passion. Temple had been content to survey the world in a smooth, stately exposition. Swift brought his arguments to England, and put them into stories which, in spite of their humorous allegory, slashed his victims with all the edges of realism. His ancients and moderns were actual warriors, brawling " on Friday last " in the King's library. His criticism was comedy.

" Virgil appeared in shining armour completely fitted to his body. He was mounted on a dapple-grey steed, the slowness of whose pace was an effect of the highest mettle and vigour. He cast his eye on the adverse wing, with a desire to find an object worthy of his valour, when, behold, upon a sorrel gelding of a monstrous size, appeared a foe issuing from among the thickest of the enemy's squadrons ; but his speed was less than his noise ; for his horse, old and lean, spent the dregs of his strength in a high trot which, though it made slow advances, yet caused a loud clashing of his armour, terrible to hear. The two cavaliers had now approached within the throw of a lance, when the stranger desired a parley, and, lifting up the vizard of his helmet, a face hardly appeared from within, which, after a pause, was known for that of the renowned Dryden. The brave Ancient suddenly started, as one possessed with surprise and disappointment together ; for the helmet was nine times too large for the head, which appeared situate far in the hinder part, even like the lady in a lobster, or like a mouse under a canopy of state, or like a shrivelled beau from within the penthouse of a modern periwig ; and the voice was suited to the visage, sounding weak and remote."

Nor did the genius of Swift surpass the talent of Temple only by the reach of drama over debate. Temple, speaking of the wits, had said : " But the last maim given to learning has been by the scorn of pedantry, which the shallow, the superficial, and the sufficient among scholars first drew to themselves, and very justly " . . . and then he had gone on to a mild simile of an infection in a town from which everybody stayed away. Swift, starting at the same point, with the compliment of imitation, made Temple look like the moon in the same sky with the sun : " But the greatest maim given to that general reception which the writings of our society have formerly received (next to the transitory state of all sublunary things) has been a superficial vein among many readers of the present age, who will by no means be persuaded to inspect beyond the surface and the rind of things ; whereas, wisdom is a fox, who, after long hunting, will at last cost you the pains to dig out. It is a cheese, which, by how much the richer, has the thicker, the homelier, and the coarser coat ; and whereof, to a judicious palate, the maggots are the best. It is a sack-posset, wherein the deeper you go you will find it the sweeter. Wisdom is a hen, whose cackling we must value and consider because it is attended with an egg. But then lastly, it is a nut, which, unless you choose with judgment, may cost you a tooth and pay you with nothing but a worm."

Temple, reflective over " the vein of ridiculing all that is serious and good, all honour and virtue, as well as learning and piety," had written a polite essay. Swift actively declared a war. His satires were like a tub thrown by seamen to a whale to keep it off the ship. Let the yelping wits and empty scholars butt and tumble the satires instead of harming the common-wealth.

The *Battle of the Books* was a bagatelle, humorously secret about the outcome of the skirmish. So, too, the *Tale of a Tub* did not trouble to complete the story of Peter and Martin and Jack, the three brothers who stood for the Church of Rome, the Church of England, and the Dissenting churches. Swift still lacked, or was too unconcerned to use, the art which insists upon thorough and finished structure. Broken meats, he might have said, were fit enough for dogs. The tale itself, satirizing the abuses of religion, made up no more than a third of the whole book. The digressions, on the abuses of learning, were the larger and more varied part. Swift had been a scholar longer than he had been a clergyman.

It was his duty to defend his Church by cutting

down its enemies. He was ruthless with the quibbles of theology, fanaticism, superstition, priestly greed and imposture. But he felt a more seasoned malice when he turned aside to prune and lop among the charlatans of wit whom he regarded as his own enemies. The strutting poets, the confident blind critics, the mercenary adulators and detractors, the treatise-mongers, the multipliers of dedications and prefaces and compendiums and commentaries and annotations and indexes, the proudly obscure writers : all these he ridiculed by the contemptuous device of praising them. Yet they were for him, at most, annoying creatures that he studied briefly before he trod on them. They had roused only his irritation. His hate, which after years of brooding had finally found the language natural to it, was for human life at large.

Temple had said, with a melancholy cadence : " When all is done, human life is, at the greatest and best, but like a froward child that must be played with and humoured a little to keep it quiet till it falls asleep, and then the care is over."

Swift saw mankind with a colder eye. " If we take an examination of what is generally understood by happiness, as it has respect either to the understanding or the senses, we shall find that all its properties and adjuncts will herd under this short definition, that it is a perpetual possession of being well deceived. And, first, with relation to the mind or understanding, 'tis manifest what mighty advantages fiction has over truth ; and the reason is just at our elbow, because imagination can build nobler scenes and produce more

46

wonderful revolutions than fortune or nature will be at expense to furnish. . . . Again, if we take this defini-tition of happiness and examine it with reference to the senses, it will be acknowledged wonderfully adapt. How fading and insipid do all objects accost us that are not conveyed in the vehicle of delusion ! How shrunk is everything as it appears in the glass of nature ! So that if it were not for the assistance of artificial mediums, false lights, refracted angles, varnish, and tinsel, there would be a mighty level in the felicity and enjoyments of mortal men." Credulity, he argued, is better than curiosity, and it is better to accept the surfaces of life with the senses than to inquire deeper with the reason. " Last week I saw a woman flayed, and you will hardly believe how much it altered her person for the worse. . . . He that can, with Epicurus, content his ideas with the films and images that fly off upon his senses from the superficies of things ; such a man, truly wise, creams off nature, leaving the sour and the dregs for philosophy and reason to lap up. This is the sublime and refined point of felicity called the possession of being well deceived ; the serene peaceful state of being a fool among knaves."

To this judgment Swift had arrived at thirty in the shadow of Temple at Moor Park. The neat aim and witty sting of his sentences had less to do with his effects than the mind and passion which showed through his clear, hard words. What he said he meant, not partly but wholly ; not with the momentary earnestness of a gesture but with the deep sincerity of a belief rooted in his constitution by his nature and his experience.

If ever Temple noticed the tiger in his garden he must have wondered. He might have asked whether it would not be wiser for Swift to smile at the childish world, and humour it till it slept. And Swift might have answered that it was beyond a tiger to look like a lamb with its soft wool, or sound like a lamb with its timid bleat, or skip like a lamb with its happy legs. Those were the lamb's gifts. If the lamb was able to lead a cheerful life in a world of butchers, then it had the gift of being well deceived. But a tiger's gifts were stripes and roars and claws angrier than swords. They did not carry with them the other gift of being deceived by butchers. The lamb could be caged, and would grow tame ; it could be starved, and would die pitifully. But if the tiger were caged or starved it would strike back with all its deadly sinews. To ask a tiger to be serene in its trap and peaceful towards its captors was simply to ask it to be a lamb. It must be a tiger still.

The dry years of Swift's dependence upon Temple came to an end with Temple's death in January 1699. The satires had not yet been published, and Swift left Farnham for London with none of the reputation which they were to bring him. At Farnham, or soon in London, he wrote out a set of resolutions to warn him when he should be old, as he had lately seen his patron. Most of the resolutions were civil enough. He would not, he resolved, be severe with young people or force his company on them, as he would force on no

48

one his advice or anecdotes. He would not be peevish, morose, suspicious, covetous, untidy, garrulous, boastful, positive, opinionative, or open to gossip or flattery. He would not be scornful of current ways or wits or fashions or men. He would not marry a young woman. In all these he might have been any young man taking prudent notes.

But in one of the resolutions he suddenly became Swift. " Not to be fond of children, or let them come near me hardly." Stella had been a child. Had she, coming near him as a child, grown to be what made him feel that other children might also trouble him ? Or was his resolution only a symptom of his general misanthropy, now so wary that it would not let mankind approach, even in its least hostile form, for fear of a weakening influence on the integrity of his hate ? At least he had learned, however he loved the one, to hate the many. His whole history lay in the seed of that antithesis.

III

VICAR AND WIT

I

JOSEPH ADDISON, that year setting out to fit himself for service to England by travelling on the Continent, could have told Swift, if he had known him, how to rise in their world. Addison had lived on at Oxford into a fellowship. He had paid court to Dryden, and by Dryden had been recommended to Jacob Tonson the bookseller, and by Tonson to Congreve, and by Congreve to Charles Montague, Chancellor of the Exchequer, and by Montague to Somers, the Lord Chancellor, and by Somers to the King. At the University ready to take orders, the expectant parson had yielded to the claims of Montague upon those accomplishments and virtues which, Montague told the head of Addison's college, were needed to offset the current depravity and corruption.

Dexterous in Latin and English verse, Addison was even more dexterous in his virtues. Though vain enough, he was not proud. He demanded little besides a reasonable prosperity and comfortable homage. He felt no anger because men were slow in recognizing merits which he had not yet shown. He did not too much mind playing at success as it was then played.

He saw little repugnant in the rules and admired the winners. It had never struck him that the world was ruled by knaves ; it had never struck him that only fools could be happy. Having taken what he found for what it was usually said to be, he was shortly to begin his travels with the approval, and at the expense, of his country.

Swift, with more genius than Addison, had less talent for success. In 1697 he had, presumably on the advice of Temple, put his hopes on the Earl of Sunderland, already tottering though still Lord Chamberlain. " My Lord Sunderland fell and I with him," Swift wrote a few weeks later. " Since that there have been other courses, which if they succeed I shall be proud to own the methods, or if otherwise, very much ashamed." All these schemes, whatever they were, had failed. With Temple dead, Swift had to trust to the Earl of Romney to urge upon the King the preferment which Temple had promised to obtain for his secretary. Romney, a friend to William in Holland before the Revolution, and supposed to have been " the great wheel on which the Revolution rolled," turned out to have, Swift said, " not a wheel to turn a mouse." " After long attendance in vain," which was what Swift called a fruitless four or five months, he again went back to Ireland, in June 1699, chaplain and temporary secretary to the Earl of Berkeley, one of the Lords Justices.

Dublin was as disappointing as London. Berkeley refused to make Swift permanent secretary on the ground that he was a clergyman, and soon afterwards further refused to appoint him Dean of Derry on the ground that he was too young. The man who had found Kilroot unendurable was in February 1700 assigned to another rustic living, at Laracor, seventeen miles from Dublin. Nor did it console him that he was made a prebendary of St. Patrick's Cathedral, Dublin, and a doctor of divinity of Dublin University in February 1701. With all his pride and all his powers, he had been sent to what he thought a shabby garrison on an unimportant frontier of the Church.

His circumstances seemed now more interesting to Varina, still unmarried at Belfast. She wrote him a letter. He answered it in a language as cold as any that ever ended what had begun as a flirtation.

" You would know what gave my temper that sudden turn," he said, " as to alter the style of my letters since I last came over. If there has been that alteration you observe, I have told you the cause abundance of times. I had used a thousand endeavours and arguments to get you from the company and place you are in ; both on account of your health and humour, which I thought were like to suffer very much in such air and before such examples. All I had in answer from you was nothing but a great deal of arguing, and sometimes in a style so imperious as I thought might have been spared, when I reflected how much you had been in the wrong. The other thing you would know is whether this change of style be owing to the thoughts of a new mistress. I declare, upon the word of a Christian and gentleman, it is not ; neither had I ever thoughts of being married to any other person but yourself." The cause of his change, he explained, was her indifference to his wishes and his opinions, particularly about her family. " I think . . . that no young woman in the world of the same income would dwindle away her health and life in such a sink and among such family conversation. Neither have all your letters been once able to persuade me that you have the least value for me, because you so little regarded what I so often said upon that matter. . . . I think I have more cause to resent your desires of me in that case than you have to be angry at my refusals " —his refusals, it appears, to endure the Warings. " If you like such company and conduct, much good do you with them ! My education has been otherwise."

At the same time, he would tell her what he had told his uncle Adam in response to an inquiry which Swift implied had come circuitously from Varina : " that if your health and my fortune were as they ought, I would prefer you above all your sex ; but that, in the present condition of both, I thought it was against your opinion, and would certainly make you unhappy ; that, had you any other offers which your friends or yourself thought more to your advantage, I should think I were very unjust to be an obstacle in your way." Since, however, her letter had showed her satisfied with his fortune, nothing now stood in the way of their felicity but her health. Nothing, that is, except his terms, which he reduced to questions.

" Are you in a condition to manage domestic affairs, with an income of less perhaps than three hundred pounds a year ? Have you such an inclination to my person and humour as to comply with my desires and way of living and endeavour to make us both as happy as you can ? Will you be ready to engage in those methods I shall direct for the improvement of your mind, so as to make us entertaining company for each other, without being miserable when we are neither visiting nor visited ? Can you bend your love and esteem and indifference to others the same way as I do mine ? Shall I have so much power in your heart, or you so much government of your passions, as to grow in a good humour upon my approach, though pro-voked by a ——? Have you so much good nature as to endeavour by soft words to smooth any rugged humour occasioned by the cross accidents of life ? Shall the place wherever your husband is thrown be more welcome than courts or cities without him ? In short, these are some of the necessary methods to please men who, like me, are deep-read in the world ; and to a person thus made I should be proud in giving all due returns towards making her happy. These are the questions I have always resolved to propose to her with whom I meant to pass my life ; and whenever you can heartily answer them in the affirmative I shall be blessed to have you in my arms, without regarding whether your person be beautiful or your fortune large. Cleanliness in the first and competency in the other is all I look for. . . . I singled you out at first from the rest of women ; and I expect not to be used like a common lover. When you think fit to send me an answer to this without ——, I shall then approve myself, by all means you shall command, Madam, your most obedient humble servant."

It was as if a glacier had announced the course it meant to take down its valley. Swift possibly disliked the Warings no more than other men have disliked their prospective relatives. His terms were possibly no more ruthless than the assumptions on which other men have entered into marriage. But few men besides Swift can ever, in such a situation, have been so revealing and so unsparing. Varina had entertained him at tedious Kilroot. She had not known how to give up the roundabout arts of courtship for the forthright sciences of marriage. Her caution had humiliated him. Her advances now embarrassed him. Himself long past the time of languishing, he turned the truth loose upon the coquette. And Varina, who had, as Swift said of young ladies in general, spent her time in making a net instead of a cage, had had the misfortune to incur the frankness of the one man then alive who could put the most naked truth into the most naked words.

If Swift struck too hard for the occasion, it was no more than his dire intensity often forced him to do. His letter at least closed the episode. Varina, with these words before her, could understand that she was not dealing with a common lover, or with a lover at all.

A man who could demand so much of a wife, and say so to a woman, was no longer at any point in a man's life where the odds are still on his marrying. About marriage Swift was frequently explicit. At twenty-five he declared that, to say nothing of his "cold temper and unconfined humour," "the very ordinary observations I made with going half a mile beyond the University have taught me experience enough not to think of marriage till I settle my fortune in the world, which I am sure will not be in some years ; and even then myself I am so hard to please that I suppose I shall put it off to the other world. . . . Among all the young gentlemen that I have known to have ruined themselves by marrying, which I assure you is a great number, I have made this general rule, that they are either young, raw, ignorant scholars who, for want of knowing company, believe every silk petti-coat includes an angel, or else they have been a sort of honest young men who perhaps are too literal in rather marrying than burning. . . . I think I am very far excluded from listing under either of these heads. I confess I have known one or two men of sense enough who, inclined to frolics, have married and ruined them-selves out of a maggot ; but a thousand household thoughts, which always drive matrimony out of my mind whenever it chances to come there, will, I am sure, fright me from that ; besides that, I am naturally temperate, and never engaged in the contrary which usually produces those effects."

This may be taken to be the scorn of a young man who has not yet felt much desire or loneliness. But there is the later belief, cut to an axiom, that " no wise man ever married from the dictates of reason." What then could beguile Swift into marriage, when, for all his passion, he had undertaken to live as faithfully under the dictates of reason as under the orders of the Church ?

Swift, speaking of himself, seldom spoke less than the exact truth, though he often, by his harshness, said rather more. In the matter of marriage his course was, from first to last, as straight as was possible for a man fascinating to women and inclined to play with them when his powers were relaxed or his will checked. He had decided that, his fortunes being so much lower than his pride, and his health so much less than his strength, he would not marry except on some such extravagant terms as he proposed at thirty-three to Varina. He knew she would not accept them. Whether he realized it or not, he preferred his relationship with Stella to marriage with anybody else.

He turned out to prefer it to marriage with Stella. During the three or four years after he closed accounts with Varina, Swift came no doubt as near to marrying Stella as the great drive of his solitary ambition would let him. But he did not marry her, and he apparently found, as many men would find if they had the strength to test the principle, that what seems to be the need to marry, even a woman truly loved, is a panic impulse in a crisis. Swift, having survived the crisis which might have made him a husband, did not have to pay the customary price of losing the woman who might have become his wife. Stella was still the willing focus of that immense affection which turned the stare or scowl of hate to the rest of the world.

Only once more did he slip recklessly into his old amusement. Vanessa, infatuated and unceasing, threatened his solitude. He could not annihilate her with a letter or subdue her to friendship. He slackly let

the affair drag on to a dreary and then vehement end.
But still he did not break his straight course. He had
not wanted to marry. He had not had to marry. He
did not mean to marry. He had said as much to
everybody whose business it could be.

Swift might have been believed if his course, no
matter how straight, had also been usual : if he had
spent his days in a cell ; if, having failed to win some
desired woman, he had desired no other ; if he had
run from woman to woman stopping nowhere long.
Instead, he lived in the world, had as much of the
women he wanted as he wanted of them, and was in
many ways faithful to Stella. Gossip, bothered by what
is unusual in the story, has tried to make it fit some
more familiar pattern by imagining hidden circumstances which, if known, would show Swift to have
been more like ordinary men. He may have been
impotent, gossip suggests, and so avoided marriage out
of vanity. He may have had syphilis, and so avoided
marriage out of decency. He may, gossip even during
his life went so far as to guess, have married Stella
privately—without licence, witnesses, or record, when
he was Dean of St. Patrick's ! But all these arguments,
some of which have been twisted to coiling lengths,
are still the hypotheses of gossip, one as good as
another. Not one of them is as simple and sufficient
as the conclusion that Swift, whom gossips could more
easily think inadequate, dissolute, or secretive, was
only, in marriage as in other matters, extraordinary.

2

Writing to Varina in May 1700 he swore that he then had no thoughts of another mistress or of another wife. As this was not a lover's letter, this was hardly a lover's oath, and may have meant what it said. But, as chaplain to Lord Berkeley, Swift was still, in a sense, a dependent ; and at Laracor he saw he would be lonely. Of his three livings, Laracor and the incidental Agher and Rathbeggan, only Laracor had a church. Swift, arriving dejected and resentful, found himself doubtfully master of a scattered, monotonous territory with a dilapidated church and a vicarage and glebe not then fit to live in. The one pleasant thing about his post was that he could leave his duties in the hands of curates and himself live much of the time in Dublin lodgings. In April 1701 he went with Berkeley back to England, to remain there till September. And there he visited Stella at Farnham.

Her mother had married, or was to marry, another steward of Moor Park, and the daughter was living with another Temple dependent, Rebecca Dingley, on the income of a Temple legacy. " Her fortune," as Swift told the story on the bitter, truthful night of Stella's death, " at that time was in all not above fifteen hundred pounds, the interest of which was but a scanty maintenance, in so dear a country, for one of her spirit. Upon this consideration, and indeed very much for my own satisfaction, who had few friends or acquaintance in Ireland, I prevailed with her and her dear friend and companion, the other lady, to draw

59

what money they had into Ireland, a great part of their fortune being in annuities upon funds. Money was then ten per cent in Ireland, besides the advantage of turning it, and all the necessaries of life at half the price. They complied with my advice, and soon after came over ; but, I happening to continue some time longer in England, they were much discouraged to live in Dublin, where they were wholly strangers. She was at that time about nineteen years old, and her person was soon distinguished. But the adventure looked so like a frolic the censure held for some time, as if there were a secret history in such a removal ; which, however, soon blew off by her excellent conduct."

These are the known facts of Stella's removal to Ireland. Nor was her life there less prudent than her going. She and Mrs. (that is, Miss) Dingley lived ordinarily in lodgings with their own servants. When Swift was at Laracor they lived in a cottage not far away or lodged in the neighbouring village of Trim. When he was in lodgings in Dublin they lodged elsewhere in town. Only, it seems, during his absences did they economize by living in the vicarage at Laracor or in his lodgings in Dublin. The relations between Stella and Swift were unwaveringly circumspect. No one knew that he made her an allowance of fifty pounds a year. " I wonder," he wrote to a friend in 1726, " how you could expect to see Mrs. Johnson in a morning, which I, her oldest acquaintance, have not done these dozen years, except once or twice in a journey." The afternoons or evenings which he spent

Esther Johnson (Stella)

with her are said never to have been without at least
a third person.

She seldom made visits. " But her own lodgings,"
Swift said, " from before twenty years old were fre-
quented by many persons of the graver sort, who all
respected her highly, upon her good sense, good manners and conversation. . . . And indeed the greatest
number of her acquaintance was among the clergy."
At first she was extravagant, " and so continued till
about two-and-twenty ; when, by advice of some
friends, and the fright of paying large bills of tradesmen who enticed her into their debt, she began to
reflect upon her own folly."

Did Stella, prudently setting out for Ireland at
twenty, foresee so many clergymen ? Could she without
flares of rebellion give up her extravagance, even to
" avoiding all expense in clothes (which she ever despised) beyond what was merely decent ? " Had she
in her nature no veins of natural folly waiting to be
uncovered ? Was there in her no longing for unreason-
able adventures ?

So far as marriage was concerned she knew, before
too long, where Swift stood. Another of her clergymen, William Tisdall, himself began to court Stella.
Finding how much authority Swift had with her,
Tisdall wrote to him, then in London, hinting, it seems,
that Swift had used his power in behalf of his own
designs. Swift's answer, in April 1704, left no doubt
in Tisdall, nor in Stella, to whom Tisdall must have
shown it.

" I will, upon my conscience and honour, tell you

the naked truth. First, I think I have said to you before that, if my fortunes and humour served me to think of that state, I should certainly, among all persons on earth, make your choice, because I never saw that person whose conversation I utterly valued but hers. This was the utmost I ever gave way to. And, secondly, I must assure you sincerely that this regard of mine never once entered into my head to be an impediment to you ; but I judged it would, perhaps, be a clog to your rising in the world ; and I did not conceive you were then rich enough to make yourself and her happy and easy. But that objection is now quite removed by what you have at present. . . . I declare I have no other ; nor shall any consideration of my own misfortune of losing so good a friend and companion as her prevail on me against her interest and settlement in the world, since it is held so necessary and convenient a thing for ladies to marry ; and that time takes off from the lustre of virgins in all other eyes but mine."

Swift insisted that he had done nothing to stand in Tisdall's way, and that he had indeed thought the affair too far along to be broken off ; " since I supposed the town had got it in their tongues, and therefore I thought it could not miscarry without some disadvantage to the lady's credit. I . . . must add that though it hath come in my way to converse with persons of the first rank, and that sex, more than is usual to men of my level and of our function, yet I have nowhere met with a humour, a wit, or conversation so agreeable, a better portion of good sense, or a truer judgment of men and things. I mean here in England, for as to the ladies of Ireland I am a perfect stranger. . . . I give you joy of your good fortunes, and envy very much your prudence and temper, and love of peace and settlement ; the reverse of which has been the great uneasiness of my life, and is like to continue so. And what is the result ? . . . I find nothing but the good words and wishes of a decayed Ministry, whose lives and mine will probably wear out before they can serve either my little hopes or their own ambition. Therefore I am resolved suddenly to retire, like a discontented courtier, and vent myself in study and speculation, till my own humour or the scene here shall change."

This was the same language as that Swift used after Stella's death, when he called her " the truest, most virtuous and valuable friend that I or perhaps any other person ever was blessed with," and said he could not remember that he had " ever once heard her make a wrong judgment of persons, books, or affairs." He could then say also, out of his long experience, that she was " the most disinterested mortal I ever knew or heard of." But his praise was for her intellectual, moral, and social virtues, as it had always been. Not a surviving syllable about her suggests desire. None comes nearer to it than his words that " she had a gracefulness somewhat more than human in every motion, word, and action." And they were written for posterity when she was dead, not when she was twenty-three and he faced a rival.

Stella, scrutizing the letter to Tisdall, could no more find a possible husband there than Varina had found in her letter four years earlier. Tisdall, however, was rejected.

And not a surviving syllable from Stella tells whether she knew of any barrier between her and Swift except the cold sword of his ambitious pride, or whether she struggled against fitting herself to the place he made for her, or whether she ever felt bitterness or regret. The discretion as native to her as to Swift protected her almost entirely from scandal, even in the mouths of his most loquacious enemies. He alone was blamed, for leaving her alone. Stella seems not to have blamed him. She preferred what she had of Swift to all she might have had of Tisdall or any other possible husband.

She knew that Swift's devotion was partly his pride admiring itself in its glass. He trusted her judgment, which was a bright reflection of his own. He took her advice, which was coloured by what she deftly guessed to be his will. But she was no such replica in dough as might have bored him or might have shamed him into guilt for using her as he did. She was witty and lively, talked back to him, was charmingly perverse when he convinced her of her errors, and would not allow him to have a maid or housekeeper " with a tolerable face." Stella gave him, when he was resisted elsewhere, the comfort of feeling over her that power without which his temper could not live. She saw, however, that she was a need as well as a comfort. She could feel an occasional thrill of power in her general peace of compliance.

For nearly a decade after Stella went to Ireland the record is so silent about her that she has to be guessed at. Then for three years during which Swift wrote his journal to her, his light brings her to life. After that, silence and obscurity, seldom broken till the light shines again in Swift's grief over her last illness. She hardly lives except in his words.

Once, however, Swift's mirror answered him. It was in an exchange of verses between them when she had been for twenty years his closest friend. His verses showed how little time had taken from her lustre in his eyes. He had never " admitted love a guest," but he could imagine nothing beyond what he had had from their friendship.

> " *In all the habitudes of life,*
> *The friend, the mistress, and the wife,*
> *Variety we still pursue,*
> *In pleasure seek for something new ;*
> *Or else, comparing with the rest,*
> *Take comfort that our own is best. . . .*
> *But his pursuits are at an end*
> *Whom Stella chooses for a friend.*"

And Stella, with verses of her own on Swift's birthday, answered him in kind. It was " your pupil and your humble friend " who congratulated him. The sum of her praise was that he had taught her to value her mind more than her person.

> " *When men began to call me fair,*
> *You interposed your timely care.*
> *You early taught me to despise*
> *The ogling of a coxcomb's eyes ;*
> *Showed where my judgment was misplaced ;*
> *Refined my fancy and my taste.*"

E   65

Now, Stella gratefully assured him, she had a better fate than that of women " with no endowments but a face."

> " *You taught how I might youth prolong,*
> *By knowing what was right and wrong ;*
> *How from my heart to bring supplies*
> *Of lustre to my fading eyes ;*
> *How soon a beauteous mind repairs*
> *The loss of changed or falling hairs ;*
> *How wit and virtue from within*
> *Send out a smoothness o'er the skin.*
> *Your lectures could my fancy fix,*
> *And I can please at thirty-six.*"

Yet in this reasonable tribute Stella let her rhyme coax her into a favourable prevarication. She was not thirty-six, but forty. She would still give herself a slight advantage when she pronounced her judgment on the frailty of beauty, which she had to endure, Swift only to observe. He had been, as she said, her early and her only guide. After so many years her verses and her words were, as much as her handwriting, like his. But with a betraying phrase she could still show a tenderness for that person which her philosopher had taught her to value less than her mind.

3

The conquest of Stella, absolute and lasting, gave Swift his only relief from his ambition. His outward life during these ten years in Ireland need not have been hateful to him if his pride had left him free to enjoy it. The income from his livings was perhaps not much over two hundred pounds a year, but it enabled him to rebuild the vicarage at Laracor and to lay out a garden. He had a stream straightened to resemble a canal and a willow-walk where he might remember Moor Park as Temple had remembered Holland. The parish duties were so light that Swift could consider Laracor, Agher, and Rathbeggan as hardly more than sinecures, of which he took the pay and left the work to deputies. In Dublin, where besides being a prebendary of the Cathedral, he was, after Berkeley's recall, chaplain to the Duke of Ormond and the Earl of Pembroke, Lord-Lieutenants, Swift was domestically allied with the rulers of the kingdom. Moreover, he was only once long out of England. He travelled back and forth over the anxious bridge of his expectations. In London he published the letters, essays, and memoirs which Temple had left to him. And there he soon took a commanding though scornful rank among the wits he ridiculed.

Swift always valued conversation, " so useful and innocent a pleasure, so fitted for every period and condition of life, and so much in all men's power." He went to such coffee-houses as the Whig St. James's and the more neutral Will's. But he never thought of himself as belonging with the general army of the wits. " The worst conversation I ever remember to have heard in my life," he said, " was that at Will's coffee-house, where the wits (as they were called) used formerly to assemble. That is to say, five or six men who had writ plays, or at least prologues, or had share in a miscellany, came thither and entertained one another with their trifling composures, in so important an air as if they had been the noblest efforts of human nature or that the fate of kingdoms depended on them. And they were usually attended with an humble audience of young students from the inns of court or the universities, who, at due distance, listened to these oracles and returned home with great contempt for their law and philosophy, their heads filled with trash, under the name of politeness, criticism, and *belles lettres.*"

If now and then Swift unbent his powers and talked in clubs, played at cold hoaxes, or wrote verse, no longer Pindaric, it was in the mood of idleness which had formerly turned him to flirtations. His successes came not from the pains he took but from the natural skill of his strong mind set to work at trifles. He moved among the wits proudly, somewhat gigantic, somewhat ominous.

His interests were in public affairs, in the government of the realm, in the whole behaviour of mankind. He began to write about politics while he was still chaplain to Berkeley. The Lords and Commons were in abusive conflict. Large tracts of land in Ireland having been forfeited to the Crown after the Revolution, the King had made grants of it to his favourites and to a former mistress. In 1700 the Commons had voted to annul these grants and to make other grants to other favourites. The Lords had resisted, but had finally given way. Lord Somers, the Whig leader of the Ministry, had been so displeasing to the Commons that the King had forced him to resign. The majority in the Parliament of 1701 was Tory, as was the Ministry. The Tories, blaming William and his Whig advisers for their foreign policy, impeached Somers, Portland, Orford, and Halifax (lately Addison's Charles Montague). The Lords supported the impeached peers. Swift, returning with Berkeley to England in April, saw in the conflict a danger to the state, and undertook a warning. He was still so near Moor Park that he came only slyly into the open in his discourse, full of modern parallels, on the dissensions between the nobles and commons in Athens and Rome.

But he wrote less like a philosopher than like a governor, contemptuous of political metaphysics. No doubt there ought to be a proper balance of power among the forces in a state ; " although I should think that the saying *vox populi vox dei* ought to be understood of the universal bent and current of a people, not of the bare majority of a few representatives, which is often procured by little arts and great industry and application ; wherein those who engage in the pursuits of malice and revenge are much more sedulous than such as would prevent them." How the universal bent and current of a people was to be recognized and encouraged Swift did not make plain. " Some physicians have thought that if it were practicable to keep the several humours of the body in an exact and equal balance of each with the opposite, it might be immortal ; and so perhaps would a political body if the balance of power could be always held exactly even. But, I doubt, this is as impossible in practice as the other."

In practice he found the populace always greedy and slippery. " When a child grows easy and content by being humoured ; and when a lover becomes satisfied by small compliances, without further pursuits ; then expect to find popular assemblies content with small concessions." " I think it is an universal truth that the people are much more dexterous at pulling down and setting up than at preserving what is fixed ; and they are not fonder of seizing more than their own than they are of delivering it up again to the worst bidder, with their own into the bargain. For, although in their corrupt notions of divine worship they are apt to multiply their gods, yet their earthly devotion is seldom paid to above one idol at a time, of their own creation ; whose oar they pull with less murmuring, and much more skill, than when they share the lading or even hold the helm."

There was, Swift thought, no mysterious virtue in any gathering of men. " It is hard to recollect one folly, infirmity, or vice to which a single man is subjected and from which a body of commons, either collective or represented, can be wholly exempt. For, beside that they are composed of men with all their infirmities about them, they have also the ill fortune to be generally led and influenced by the very worst among themselves, I mean popular orators, tribunes, or, as they are now styled, great speakers, leading men, and the like. Whence it comes to pass that in their results we have sometimes found the same spirit of cruelty and revenge, of malice and pride, the same blindness and obstinacy and unsteadiness, the same ungovernable rage and anger, the same injustice, sophistry, and fraud that ever lodged in the breast of any individual."

The evil to be avoided, Swift held, was the tyranny equally of the one, of the few, or of the many. But when the many are tyrants the tyranny of the one is not far off. " A usurping populace is its own dupe, a mere underworker, and a purchaser in trust for some single tyrant whose state and power they advance to their own ruin, with as blind an instinct as those worms that die with weaving magnificent habits for beings of a superior nature to their own."

Any governor, reading Swift's discourse, must have felt behind it a congenial mind and will. Swift might dread the tyranny of a king. He might even, as he later wrote, " prefer a well-instituted commonwealth before a monarchy." But what he really dreaded was disorder. " If," he said, " I should insist upon liberty of conscience, form conventicles of republicans, and print books preferring that government and condemning what is established, the magistrate would, with great justice, hang me and my disciples." Better the certain magistrate than the uncertain mob. Swift was no less on the side of power because he wanted power himself. He regarded the demand for popular rights as a king might regard it : that is, as a mode of usurpation. He regarded the prospect of revolution as a general might regard it : that is, as a threat of mutiny. Let theorists be hanged. Though the end of government was liberty, the way to it did not lead through

71

unrest. Unrest was itself the tyranny of the many, and it might at any time become the tyranny of the one. Liberty lay between these extremes. Mankind, unless it gave itself to dictatorship or to confusion, had to be governed by the few.

Not, however, by the casual few of birth or wealth. By the chosen few of knowledge, skill, and virtue. Swift did not say, at first or ever, how these few were to be chosen. Like all the men, in all the ages, who have held to this appealing doctrine, he assumed that the choice of governors ought to be as natural as it was logical. And, like most of them, he assumed that he belonged among the governors.

Rather, he assumed that he belonged beside them. Swift had already come to think of himself as first of all a churchman, not a statesman but the driving conscience of statesmen. Having delivered his warning in his pamphlet, written in London, he left it with the printer and went back to Ireland, to establish himself in Laracor. " The book was," he says, " greedily bought and read ; and charged sometimes upon my Lord Somers and some time upon the Bishop of Salisbury." Associated at a distance with men so powerful, Swift, returning to England for the summer of 1702, and owning the authorship, came closer to the seats of power than he had ever come before. " My Lords Somers and Halifax, as well as the Bishop . . . desired my acquaintance, with great marks of esteem and professions of kindness—not to mention the Earl of Sunderland, who had been of my old acquaintance. They lamented that they were not able to serve me since the death of the King ; and were very liberal in promising me the greatest preferments I conld hope for, if ever it came in their power. I soon grew domestic with Lord Halifax, and was as often with Lord Somers as the formality of his nature (the only unconversable fault he has) made it agreeable to me."

Swift was, in his relations with the great, no country parson tickled with a dinner. He stood before them like a man there in his own right. " It was then I first began to trouble myself with the difference between the principles of Whig and Tory ; having formerly employed myself in other and, I think much better, speculations. I talked often upon this subject with Lord Somers ; told him that, having been long con-versant with the Greek and Roman authors, and therefore a lover of liberty, I found myself much inclined to be what they called a Whig in politics ; and that, besides, I thought it impossible, upon any other principle, to defend or submit to the Revolution. But as to religion I confessed myself to be a high churchman, and that I did not conceive how any one who wore the habit of clergyman could be otherwise." A high churchman, and a haughty one. Though he might then prefer the Whigs to the Tories, his real allegiance was to the Church. He served it when he served whatever party favoured it. He was above the battle in which he fought. He looked for large rewards with the assurance of his calling as well as with the arrogance of his temper.

But Somers and Halifax were not in office. Swift

went back to Ireland, unrewarded, for another year of rueful banishment.

When he once more returned to England late in 1703, he seemed, to his own pride, to have done nothing in the world. Yet he had an honourable profession. He had an income for life. He had a mistress, of a kind, who was young, beautiful, witty, and devoted. He had ruling friends in Ireland and was beginning to have others in England. He was the author of the most brilliant prose satire so far written in English, and the master of the best prose of his age. Something boundless in him, however, or something perverse, kept him from more than brief satisfactions. Content to be a clergyman, he could not wait to be a bishop. Untroubled by debts, he longed for a fortune. Happy with Stella for a friend, he would not commit himself to her in marriage. A scholar, a clergyman, and a wit, he cared little for the company of his fellows. He thought the scholars pedantic, the clergymen dull and tattling—

> " *And deal in vices of the graver sort,*
> *Tobacco, censure, coffee, pride, and port* "—

the wits frivolous and feeble. His satires had remained for half a dozen years unpublished. He could be at ease only among the great, and even there he did not lend himself wholly to their purposes. He stood solitary on the peak of his own nature, his scornful eyes raking mankind.

From this height he flung down his *Tale of a Tub* early in 1704. Mankind at large took no notice. Man-

kind at large has no eyes to read with, no skin to feel
a lash with. As Swift himself said in his preface,
" Satire, being levelled at all, is never resented for an
offence by any, since every individual person makes
bold to understand it of others, and very wisely removes
his particular part of the burden upon the shoulders of
the world, which are broad enough, and able to bear
it." Nor did the pedants and wits flinch at his thrusts
much more sharply, since he named few of them, than
the nameless run of men. The pedants might grumble,
but the wits, who also liked to sting, could take a
craftsman's pleasure in the accurate rapture of his
stinging.

Swift of course pricked no active folly and stabbed
no active vice by his satires. Fools did not read him.
Wise men were only confirmed in their wisdom. His
hatred caused less reformation than delight. The
delight which men felt in his arguments and allegories,
so cutting, so copious, so downright, so fanciful, was the
delight which men feel when one of them uses words as
most of them have not the gift to do, only the bursting
desire. Swift, who scorned to be a man of words, was
accepted for his words. Somers, to whom the book was
dedicated, and Halifax, who knew how to put such
skill as Swift's to use, repeated their promises. They
did not tell him it was not his counsel that they needed.

Yet while he was making friends he was also making
enemies. Mankind was not a sensitive body, able to
feel in any of its parts any indignity to the whole. The
pedants or the wits were not. The Church was. It
thought of itself as marked off from the world, like its

75

consecrated altars, to be approached with reverence. There were, as Swift contended, abuses of religion which called for satire, and which could be satirized without any hurt to true religion. But the line between the uses and the abuses of religion was often faint. One man's devotion could be another man's fanaticism. Firmness could become stoniness and never know it. Laughter, even when aimed at what was false, could wound in two directions. Swift, high on his peak of scorn, let his laughter fall with a harsh inclusiveness.

When, for instance, he touched the doctrine of transubstantiation, he traced its origin to a noisy episode in the career of the Catholic among the three brothers of the allegory. Peter, having no mutton for his dinner, served up a brown loaf to Martin and Jack. He told them it was mutton. They refused, at first politely and then heatedly, to believe him. " Look ye, gentlemen," cries Peter in a rage, " to convince you what a couple of blind, positive, ignorant, wilful puppies you are, I will use but this plain argument : By G——, it is true, good, natural mutton as any in Leadenhall market ; and G—— condemn you both eternally if you believe otherwise." Such a thundering proof as this left no further room for objection.

Here was rough language to use so near the communion table, no matter what the precise beliefs of the bystanders regarding the disputed miracle. A total unbeliever could not have spoken more gratingly. Even in that vigorous age a clergyman had to watch his voice if he was to become a bishop. Swift might please the lords temporal with his originality and force, but he could not please the lords spiritual without orthodoxy and decorum. Within the Church he was always, from the time *A Tale of a Tub* was understood to be by him, a churchman suspected of irreverence—or, as he phrased it, " the sin of wit."

This dangerous book, published with mystifying stealth, Swift never acknowledged, though after a scuffle of ascriptions it settled down at his door. The authorship was first his humorous and afterwards his cautious secret. When, having published the satires, he followed his letter to Tisdall back to Ireland, he was still barely known in London for his genius. There are almost no records of where he had lodged, of how he had spent his days and nights. A dim figure, flashing seldom out of the dark.

One anecdote, of the many which have gathered about his magnetic reputation, may tell something like the truth. For days after his earliest appearance at the St. James's coffee-house, the story goes, he did not speak. He would come in, lay his hat on a table, walk conspicuously up and down the room for an hour, take up his hat, pay his money at the bar, and leave without a word. At last, one evening, he looked several times at a man in boots, who seemed to have just come from the country. The mad parson, as he was already called, went up to the booted stranger and said abruptly : " Pray, Sir, do you remember any good weather in the world ? " The man stared but said he thanked God he could remember a great deal of good weather. " That is more," said Swift, " than I can say. I never remember any weather that was not too hot or too cold, too wet or too dry. But, however God Almighty contrives it, at the end of the year 'tis all very well." Then again he took his hat and left.

The next three and a half years in Ireland saw him more at ease with more companions. At Laracor he planted, besides willows, holly, apple, cherry trees. He fished for eel and pike and trout. " I carry double the flesh that you saw about me at London," he wrote to John Temple, who had invited him to revisit Moor Park in 1706 ; though Swift insisted that he had, to such a sign of fortune, " no manner of title, having neither purchased it by luxury nor good humour." His congregation might be no more than fifteen persons, " most of them gentle and all simple," but he had numerous friends in the region of Laracor.

In Dublin he could talk clerical politics with the Primate of Ireland and the Archbishop of Dublin, both Swift's friends, and secular politics with the Lord-Lieutenants to whom he was chaplain. At the Castle he was cheerful with the successive households of Ormond and Pembroke. With a small circle of Pembroke's intimate guests he punned tumultuously and infectiously. He drank wine, took snuff, and gambled for trifling stakes. He was often at the house of the Dean of St. Patrick's, who gave good dinners to bishops and to clergymen willing to become bishops. There was also a sort of club with which various women, Stella among them, met on Saturday evenings, for dinner and ombre or picquet. Stella was liked and admired by Swift's friends. If he was lonely and restless he had his genius to blame.

4

He was lonely and steadily more restless. The idyll of Laracor was too mild to hold him. The work and play of Dublin were too small. Just before his fortieth birthday he left Ireland, in the party of Lord Pembroke, again to try at fortune on fortune's own ground. He had at least the advantage, now, of being on an official errand to the great men whose favour he personally needed. Commissioned by his Archbishop, he was to act as lobbyist in the matter of the First Fruits. Queen Anne, devoted to the interests of the Church, had given up her right to the first year's income of every ecclesiastical benefice in England. The Irish Church hoped she would extend the same bounty to Ireland. The whole sum at issue was not above a thousand pounds a year. Swift, proud as a mountain, took up the little cause. It brought him a new experience of the delaying, forgetting, bargaining habits of politicians.

He had to move softly to avoid the jealousy of Pembroke, who as Viceroy of Ireland was the proper channel for any such appeal to the Crown. At first Somers, though influential with the Ministry, was still out of office. He referred Swift to Sunderland, son of Swift's former friend, son-in-law of Marlborough, and a Secretary of State. Sunderland said he would go with Swift to Godolphin, Lord Treasurer, but ended by merely making an appointment. Godolphin declared " he was passive in this business," which was really Pembroke's responsibility. Swift consulted Pembroke, and was told that everything depended on the Queen.

Passed shiftily from hand to hand, Swift saw that none of the great men was interested, though none of them would take the trouble to tell the truth. After a year he heard from Pembroke that the grant had been made, and a little later learned that Pembroke had lied. But the Earl of Wharton had been appointed Lord-Lieutenant. Swift went to Wharton, " which was the first attendance I ever paid him." Wharton had nothing for him but cloudy excuses and windy promises. " I took the boldness to begin answering those objections, and designed to offer some reasons ; but he rose suddenly, turned off the discourse, and seemed in haste ; so I was forced to take my leave." At a subsequent meeting at Somers's house Wharton " received me as dryly as before."

Thereafter Swift hated Wharton as he never hated another man. All the exasperations of a wasted year came together into a single fury which, when Swift had a chance, poured itself out into the abuse which has made Wharton better known for it than for all he ever did himself.

Lobbying for the First Fruits, Swift looked out also for his own advancement. But he went through his visit to England always in suspense and never satisfied. First he hoped to be chosen Bishop of Waterford. He believed he had the favour of Somers and possibly of the Archbishop of Canterbury and the Queen. Another clergyman of the Pembroke circle was preferred. " Now I must retire to my morals," Swift wrote a friend, " and pretend to be wholly without ambition and to resign with patience. . . . And after this if you

will not allow me to be a good courtier, I will pretend
to it no more. But let us talk no further on this subject.
I am stomach-sick of it already." Then he hoped to be
sent as secretary to Vienna, if Lord Berkeley should go
as ambassador. " I shall be out of the way of parties
until it shall please God I have some place to retire
to a little above contempt." The Ministry promised
Swift the post, but Berkeley's age and ill health kept
him in England. Swift would have accepted a Dublin
parish which had been proposed to him ; the living did
not fall vacant. He might have been expected to be
chaplain to Wharton, as he had been to Ormond and
Pembroke ; he was not chosen. He was urged by the
Archbishop of Dublin to try for the deanery of Down ;
Wharton's chaplain became dean. On the day, after
Swift's return to Ireland, when the Bishop of Cork was
dying of spotted fever Swift wrote to Halifax asking for
his interest with Somers, now Lord President, for this
bishopric. Wharton, according to Swift, engaged his
credit to get the place for a clergyman who had married
a " cast wench " of Wharton's—although the Queen,
indeed, prevented such a scandal. To make the story
as complete as a farce, the clergyman in question may
have been that junior dean of Trinity College before
whom, on his knees, Swift on his twenty-first birthday
may have had to beg pardon for being contemptuous
and contumacious.

Yet towards the close of his cycle of anxiety Swift
could write ingratiatingly to Halifax : " I must take
leave to reproach your Lordship for a most inhuman
piece of cruelty, for I can call your extreme good usage

of me no better, since it has taught me to hate the place
where I am banished, and raised my thoughts to an
imagination that I might live to be some way useful or
entertaining if I were permitted to live in town. . . . I
have been studying how to be revenged of your Lordship, and have found out the way. They have in
Ireland the same idea with us, of your Lordship's
generosity, magnificence, wit, judgment, and knowledge in the enjoyment of life. But I shall quickly un-
deceive them by letting them plainly know that you
have neither interest nor fortune which you can call
your own ; both having been long made over to the
corporation of deserving men in want, who have
appointed you their advocate and steward, which the
world is pleased to call patron and protector. I shall
inform them that myself and about a dozen others kept
the best table in England, to which because we admitted your Lordship in common with us, made you
our manager, and sometimes allowed you to bring a
friend, therefore ignorant people would needs take
you to be the owner. . . . Pray, my Lord, desire Dr.
South to die about the fall of the leaf, for he has a prebend of Westminster which will make me your neighbour, and a sinecure in the country, both in the
Queen's gift, which my friends have often told me
would fit me extremely."

And Halifax could magniloquently answer : " I am
quite ashamed for myself and my friends to see you
left in a place so incapable of tasting you ; and to see
so much merit and so great qualities unrewarded by
those who are sensible of them. Mr. Addison and I are

entered into a new confederacy, never to give over the pursuit, nor to cease reminding those who can serve you, till your worth is placed in that light where it ought to shine. Dr. South holds out still, but he cannot be immortal. The situation of his prebendary would make me doubly concerned in serving you, and upon all occasions that shall offer I will be your constant solicitor, your sincere admirer, and your unalterable friend."

Handsome compliment, handsome acknowledgment, and no real confidence between the writers. What Swift actually thought of Halifax was that he gave deserving men " only good words and dinners ; I never heard him say one good thing, or seem to taste what was said by another." What Halifax actually thought of Swift must be guessed at. But no patron used to " soft dedication all day long " could quite relish a follower so bound to lead. Swift would never be as remote from politics as Newton, whom Halifax had made Warden and then Master of the Mint, nor as obliging and grateful in the midst of politics as Addison, who through Halifax had entered the busy circle where few men went long without places. Halifax and Somers and Pembroke no more than Godolphin and Sunderland and Wharton by this time could imagine in Swift's hand the supple, obedient pen which they required.

There was proof to support their doubts. They had been willing to bargain with him, or through him with the Irish Church, about the First Fruits. Let the Church consent to the repeal of the Sacramental Test which excluded Dissenters from office. The Whigs, standing to gain votes from the pleased Dissenters, would then be better able to persuade the Queen to widen her bounty. The repeal would mean only the surrender of a principle, and it would save the Irish clergy a thousand pounds a year. Swift, without a thought of accommodating the ministers or even of earning their possible rewards, had instead written too vigorously, and not surreptitiously enough, against the repeal. He saw it as a selfish experiment which England wanted to try first on Ireland before trying it nearer home. " If your little finger be sore," he said to England with a snarling humility, " and you think a poultice made of our vitals will give it any ease, speak the word and it shall be done." Somers, Lord President, and Wharton, Lord-Lieutenant, from that moment must have known that Swift was not their man. The sin of wit they could forgive, and indeed encourage. They could neither encourage nor forgive the sin of such independence. Braver statesmen than they might have hesitated to keep a tiger on the hearth.

Swift, learning on this visit to England that the great are not always to be trusted by the proud and truthful, should have become finally aware that he was not a Whig, perhaps that he was not a Tory. As a Churchman he stood not so much between the parties as above them both. " I should think," he said in one of the pamphlets in which he stretched the muscles which the ministers would not let him use, " that . . . to preserve the constitution entire in Church and State, whoever has a true value for both would be sure to avoid the extremes of Whig for the sake of the former and the extremes of Tory on account of the latter." Arbitrary power he still hated and looked upon " as a greater evil than anarchy itself ; as much as a savage is in a happier state of life than a slave at the oar." Yet his passion was, as always, for order. The legislature, he thought, could not be placed in too many hands ; the administration, however, not in too few. Sects might indeed be tolerated in a state, but " a government cannot give them too much ease nor trust them with too little power." Order, as he understood it, was the consequence of virtue among the people, and therefore a higher concern than politics could reach to. It was the natural concern of the Church.

Like a Churchman, like a magistrate, Swift proposed that manners be reformed by the advancement of religion. If the Queen should make stricter demands upon all who came near her, " morality and religion would soon become fashionable Court virtues, and be taken up as the only methods to get or keep employments there ; which alone would have mighty influence upon many of the nobility and principal gentry." The example of the Court would go far to reform the town, and the town the rest of the kingdom. " How ready . . . would most men be to step into the paths of virtue and piety if they infallibly led to favour and fortune ! " Swift could even contemplate " something parallel to the office of censors anciently in Rome," which in England he believed " could be easily limited from running into any exorbitancies." British Catos could reduce the vices of the army, the universities, the law courts, the public service, the press, the taverns. And the Church could provide the Catos if clergymen ceasing to live so largely to themselves and with each other, would " make themselves as agreeable as they can in the conversations of the world."

Nor did Swift stop with arguing soberly like a parson. He went on to irony, like a wit. He could not feel sure, he said, that Christianity had to be abolished, as the world thought. He meant, of course, " nominal Christianity, the other having been for some time wholly laid aside by general consent." Nominal Christianity had its uses. It gave men a God to revile, when otherwise they might abuse the government. It furnished each parish with at least one person who could read and write. It kept ten thousand men so poor that they were healthy, and good for the breed. It set one day in seven aside for pleasure, extra business, gallantry, and sleep. It made certain kinds of behaviour, because they were forbidden, more enticing. It gave the vulgar various pleasant superstitions with which to amuse the children and to shorten tiresome winter nights. It sustained the spirit of opposition, of eccentricity, of fanaticism. However, Swift ended, if Christianity was to be abolished, so ought every vestige of religion for fear there might still be some restraint laid on human nature. Let freedom come, even though bank stocks might fall one per cent.

5

No matter what grave words he used, Swift had to set them to witty tunes. They came, it seems, so effortlessly that he undervalued them, overlooking them in the thunder of his will. He valued only what he did not have : influence at a Court he despised, power over men he hated. Addison could call him, for his wit, " the greatest genius of his age." Swift wanted, as Addison had elsewhere rhetorically put it, to ride in the whirlwind and direct the storm. There was no help for his charging desire. His will was as truly his nature as his wit was.

Yet it was by his wit that he won his hearing, and from the coffee-houses. While he waited, impatient, for a single minister to listen to his business of the First Fruits, he amused his idleness with a hoax that ran through the town like a scandal. He predicted, in a burlesque almanac, that the astrologer John Partridge, who was a cobbler as well as a quack, would " infallibly die upon the 29th of March next, about eleven at night, of a raging fever." When the time came Swift no less circumstantially announced the death, though it had, he said, occurred four hours earlier than he had calculated. Partridge, still as much alive as ever, complained. The coffee-houses laughed. There were other pamphlets on the hoax, in one of which Congreve had a hand. For more than a year Swift now and then worried his victim. Richard Steele thought the joke so good, and the name of Isaac Bickerstaff, which Swift used, so noted, that he made the imaginary Bickerstaff the apparent editor of the *Tatler*. Another of Swift's hoaxes had a small success. Reading to the Countess of Berkeley, he had grown tired of the pompous commonplaces which soothed her in her favourite author, and had relieved his boredom by tricking her with a meditation which he had written upon a broomstick. Now the story got out, and the wits laughed at the trick and at the parody, which was seen in manuscript and may have been printed.

In both hoaxes the delighted wits felt not only Swift's comic skill but the imperious insolence which lay behind it. Here was a man whose lightest words left a mark wherever they touched. Here was a learned clergyman who, as the *Tatler* said, " writes very like a gentleman and goes to heaven with a very good mien."

Much of Swift's life during this stay in England was off the stage of the wits, nearer officials or drawing-rooms. When he first arrived he lived in Leicester Fields at the house of Sir Andrew Fountaine, who had been in Ireland with Pembroke and had found Swift the best pastime of that wilderness. Afterward in lodgings in the Haymarket, Swift might have letters sent to him at the St. James's coffee-house or at Steele's office in the Cockpit, but when he was kept indoors, as he once was by broken shins, even Somers came to visit him. During 1708 he was a guest of both Berkeley and Pembroke in the country. After the hot summer in town he spent six weeks in Kent and at Epsom, where the Court then retired to drink the fashionable waters.

In town he was often—much too often for his future peace—at the house of Mrs. Vanhomrigh, the widow of a former lord mayor of Dublin, who had come to London about the same time as Swift. She had a daughter Esther, who claimed to be two years younger than she was, and to have been born, as she probably had not, on St. Valentine's day. Through the Van-homrighs, friends of Fountaine, Swift met other women, ladies of the Court, toasts of the clubs, whom he fascinated by his grave impudence. He insisted that each lady who desired to know him should make the first advances. When Anne Long, toast of the Kit-Cat club, protested and held out, Swift drew up a formal treaty of which the plain terms, with whatever circum-locutions, were that she must within two hours make " all advances to the said Doctor that he shall de-mand . . . purely upon account of his great merit." The lady yielded. Swift might be resisted when he worked, not when he played.

He had the further comfort that Stella and Rebecca Dingley were in England for a part of his stay. " Mrs. Johnson," he wrote to Ireland, " cannot make a pun if she might have the weight of it in gold." He did not introduce her to his new acquaintances, the one Esther to the other, any more than he told the world his moody secrets. Stella was his secret. Though he saw her in London and wrote to her after she returned to Ireland, there are no records of her in his letters except a mention of her dog. " Pug is very well, and likes London wonderfully, but Greenwich better, where we could hardly keep him from hunting down the deer."

What came nearest to satisfying Swift in 1708 was Addison. When last Swift had been in London, in the winter of 1703-1704, he had been still unknown, and Addison, just back from his travels, had been, thanks to the bad fortune of the Whigs, in eclipse. Swift, leaving his satires behind him, had gone off to his banishment. Addison, writing a panegyric on Marlborough on account of Blenheim, had stayed to become famous over night. When now they met in February, Swift was still without any influence except that of his own genius, and Addison was an under-secretary of State. But there was no difference in their affections. Addison was seldom vain with Swift, whom he called " the most agreeable companion, the truest friend, and the greatest genius of his age." Swift was seldom proud with Addison. " If," he later wrote, back in Dublin, " you will come over again, when you are at leisure, we will raise an army and make you king of Ireland."

They met like princes, with exchange of gifts. Swift gave Addison, along with Steele, some of his moral fury, which they tempered to moral irony in the *Tatler* and *Spectator*, preferring to laugh, not scourge, virtue into fashion. Addison gave to Swift some of his smooth taste with which to revise the story of Baucis and Philemon which Swift had written in his gruff exile. Too proud to be stubborn about his verses, Swift, as he loosely said, let Addison " blot out fourscore, add fourscore, and alter fourscore " of the lines. The poem suffered, bus Swift did not. He would, and did, write more smoothly if it were more pleasing to Addison. In time Swift came to be aware of Addison's vanity and caution, but for months he had no reservations. Addison was Swift's first equal friend. Temple had been his teacher, Stella his pupil, his friends in Ireland mere accidental comrades, the Whig lords and bishops too great to be easy with. Addison had wit, charm, learning, virtue, " worth enough," Swift said, " to give reputation to an age."

All the spring and summer of 1708 they often dined together, at different taverns, frequently with Steele or Congreve, with Ambrose Philips, Addison's little Whig poetical friend, or with Robert Hunter, the friend of Swift who was going to be governor of Virginia and who threatened to make Swift his bishop in a country even more desolate than Ireland. But it was best when the two could, as Swift wrote to Hunter, " steal to a pint of bad wine, and wish for no third person but you." When Addison went off to Ireland as secretary to Wharton, with a salary of two thousand pounds a year and a sinecure worth four hundred more, Swift, still without promotion or much hope, felt no envy. In Ireland, when he had gone there in June 1709, he buried himself with Stella at Laracor and left it for Dublin, with its abominable Lord-Lieutenant, only to see Addison.

IV

MAN IN POWER

I

FORTUNE prefers to turn its wheel to the advantage of men with the talent for success, but now and then the geniuses, uncompromising, wilful, audacious, swing upward in the sun. A revolution of the wheel in London called Swift back in September 1710.

He did not know when he went what he was going to. He was almost resigned to Laracor and Dublin. " I never went to England with so little desire in my life," he wrote to Stella the day after he landed. " I am perfectly resolved to return as soon as I have done my commission, whether it succeeds or no." He had less hope as to the success of his errand, which again was the First Fruits, than the Irish bishops who this time had authorized him. Still, there was a chance. Sunderland and Godolphin had been shaken from their posts by an upheaval among the Whigs, and Wharton had hurried over to serve his party with his gift for wheedling and rounding up the voters. Other ministers might be more favourable to Swift's embassy. Other friends might help him to promotion.

At London he found everything " turning upside down ; every Whig in great office will, to a man, be

infallibly put out ; and we shall have such a winter as
has not been seen in England." It was already such a
September as Swift had never seen. " The Whigs were
ravished to see me," he wrote within two days of his
arrival, " and would lay hold on me as a twig while
they are drowning, and the great men making me
their clumsy apologies " for their former negligence.

But Swift had come into a new world of new men.
Somers was about to be dismissed. Halifax had only
his sinecure. Pembroke was in retirement. Wharton
was to lose his place to the Duke of Ormond. Sunderland had given way to Henry St. John (later Viscount
Bolingbroke) as principal Secretary of State. Godolphin had yielded the rank of first minister to Robert
Harley (later Earl of Oxford), Chancellor of the
Exchequer though not yet Lord Treasurer. The men
of Swift's old world were now able to do for him as little
as they had been willing to do before. Only the hated
Wharton " affected very much to caress " him. Somers
was merely plausible. Halifax moved too slowly.
Godolphin, whom Swift saw at once, was so " short,
dry, and morose " that the suitor was enraged. On his
third day in London Swift spent the evening at the
St. James's coffee-house with a friend. " For an hour
and a half we talked treason heartily against the Whigs,
their baseness and ingratitude. And I am come home
rolling resentments in my mind and framing schemes
of revenge."

In spite of the drowning Whigs, and in spite even of
Addison, again in England and at first as affectionate
as ever, Swift began to look towards the Tories. A

week, and he was dining with his old friend of Kilkenny and Trinity, Francis Stratford, a merchant who, " worth a plumb," was " lending the government forty thousand pounds." Two weeks later, and Swift expected any day to be taken to Harley by one of Stratford's friends, Erasmus Lewis, who was one of Harley's favourites. " I am already represented to Harley," Swift told Stella, " as a discontented person that was ill used for not being Whig enough ; and I hope for good usage from him. The Tories dryly tell me I may make my fortune if I please ; but I do not understand them, or rather, I do understand them."

Halifax asked Swift to dinner at Hampton Court and " would have kept me to-morrow to show me his house and park. . . . Lord Halifax began a health to me to-day. It was the resurrection of the Whigs, which I refused unless he would add their reformation too." The next night " after I had put out my candle . . . my landlady came into my room with a servant of Lord Halifax, to desire I would go dine with him " the following day. " But I sent him word I had business of great importance that hindered me. . . . And to-day I was brought privately to Mr. Harley, who received me with the greatest respect and kindness imaginable. He has appointed me an hour on Saturday at four, afternoon, when I will open my business to him."

Exactly a month after Swift reached London he handed Harley his memorial regarding the First Fruits. " Mr. Harley came out to meet me, brought me in, and presented me to his son-in-law . . . and his own son and, among others, Will Penn the Quaker.

We sat two hours, drinking . . . good wine . . . and two hours more he and I alone." Harley read Swift's memorial " and put it in his pocket to show the Queen ; . . . told me he must bring Mr. St. John . . . and me acquainted ; and spoke so many things of personal kindness and esteem for me that I am inclined half to believe what some friends have told me, that he would do everything to bring me over. . . . He has desired me to dine with him on Tuesday, and after four hours being with him set me down at St. James's coffee-house in a hackney coach. All this is odd and comical if you consider him and me. He knew my Christian name very well. . . . And now I am going in charity to send Steele a *Tatler*, who is very low of late."

Swift, writing that night to Stella, thought that even the *Tale of a Tub* might no longer be held against him, as he guessed it had been. " They may talk of the *you know what;* but, gad, if it had not been for that I should never have been able to get the access I have had ; and if that helps me to succeed, then that same thing will be serviceable to the Church."

Odd and comical. Harley, no more concerned about the bounty of the First Fruits than about the orthodoxy of the *Tale*, had set out to seduce the most lively and deadly wit in England. At the price of a thousand pounds a year, cut out of the Queen's income, Swift would be a bargain for her minister.

The minister did not lag in his pursuit. On Tuesday, presenting Swift to Sir Simon Harcourt, the Attorney-General, Harley said he had broached the matter of the First Fruits to the Queen, and asked Swift to dinner on Sunday. On Sunday Harley said the Queen had consented to the grant. Matthew Prior, a better poet than Addison, dined with them. After dinner, when Lord Peterborough had come in, the talk shifted to " a paper of verses " on Godolphin which had just been printed. " Lord Peterborough would let nobody read them but himself ; so he did ; and Mr. Harley bobbed me at every line to take notice of the beauties. Prior rallied Lord Peterborough for author of them ; and Lord Peterborough said he knew them to be his ; and Prior then turned it upon me, and I on him. I am not guessed at all in town to be the author." Lucky Tories, to blunder into such a moving compliment ? Or wily Tories, used to poets ?

There was some formal delay in the execution of the grant, but Harley was still, Swift wrote, " so excessively obliging that I know not what to make of it, unless to show the rascals of the other party that they used a man unworthily who had deserved better." St. John, using Swift " with all the kindness in the world," said he had never read anything so good as certain verses by the Tories' new poet which Swift himself did not " reckon so very good neither " ; and pleased Swift further by telling him that " Mr. Harley complained he could keep nothing from me, I had the way so much of getting into him." Erasmus Lewis tactfully hinted that Swift, not quite comfortable at leaving his old friends, might save Steele his post as commissioner of stamps. Swift went to Addison, as the discreeter person, but " party had so possessed him that he talked as if he suspected me, and would not fall in with anything I said. So I stopped short in my overture, and we parted very dryly. . . . When shall I grow wise? I endeavour to act in the most exact points of honour and conscience, and my nearest friends will not understand it so."

It was not in Swift to be patient. Two weeks later he inquired of Stella : " Why should the Whigs think I came to England to leave them ? Sure my journey was no secret. I protest sincerely I did all I could to hinder it . . . although now I do not repent it. But who the devil cares what they think ? . . . Rot 'em for ungrateful dogs. I will make them repent their usage before I leave this place." He had already begun to punish them. Before the end of October he had accepted the secret editorship of the *Examiner*, the Tory weekly which he edited, and wrote, until the following June, when, " my style being soon discovered, and having contracted a great number of enemies, I let it fall into other hands."

The step cost Swift his Whig friends. In six weeks : " Mr. Addison and I hardly meet once a fortnight." In another month : " I called at the coffee-house, where I had not been in a week, and talked coldly a while with Mr. Addison. All our friendship and dearness are off. We are civil acquaintances, talk words of course, of when we shall meet, and that's all." Not even the great affection between the two could hold Swift to the Whigs. He had never been entirely a Whig, as he was not now entirely a Tory. He was a Churchman, and the Tories had done for his Church what the Whigs had not done. He was hot for power, and the

Tories had taken him into their councils, as the Whigs had not. At last he had found something better for him than hopes : work that seemed to him important, recognition that seemed to him his due. For the first time in his life his pride was asked to what he considered fit company.

Harley's dinners were for Swift a sign that his fortunes finally stood beside his ambition. Nor was he required to argue for principles he did not believe in. The Tories were, it was easy for him to think, more truly than the Whigs the party of order in Church and State. When he had spoken his mind about the Sacramental Test a year before, the Whigs had turned away from him, as if he were a Tory, and the Archbishop of Dublin had written to ask " by what artifice did you contrive to pass for a Whig ? " Perhaps he had been a Tory. He would be a Tory. It was enough for Swift, as it had been enough when he took Orders, that he was assigned a post in a cause which he thought good. He gave to his cause all his passion, intensity, genius.

2

When Swift closed with Harley there commenced a chapter singular in history. No other man of affairs has ever made such use of a man of letters. At the outset Harley so misgauged his pamphleteer that after three months he could send him a banknote for fifty pounds. It was as if the squire had tipped the bishop. Swift was furious at " both the thing and the manner." He returned the money, refused to dine with Harley the next day, and demanded satisfaction. "If we let these great ministers pretend too much," he wrote to Stella, "there will be no governing them." A week later, still unreconciled, he went to the lobby of the House of Commons, found Harley, and sent him into the House to call St. John, "to let him know I would not dine with him if he dined late." The Chancellor of the Exchequer, soon to be Lord Treasurer, ran the errand to the Secretary of State for the vicar of Laracor. The next day Swift told Stella he had " taken Mr. Harley into favour again."

On Saturday of that week Swift was asked to dine with Harley in the company of St. John and Harcourt, now Lord Keeper, and became a member of the group which, meeting every Saturday except when the Queen was at Windsor, informally concerted the government of the realm. Swift did not come humbly to this cabinet. " Lord Rivers was got there before me, and I chid him for presuming to come on a day when only Lord Keeper, the Secretary, and I were to be there ; but he regarded me not. So we all dined together, and sat down at four ; and the Secretary has invited me to dine with him to-morrow. I told them I had no hopes they could ever keep in but that I saw they loved each other so well, as indeed they seem to do. They call me nothing but Jonathan ; and I said I believed they would leave me Jonathan, as they found me."

Bullying, rallying, Swift took and kept his seat in their councils. Together they planned the steps that were to be taken to oust the Whigs, to get rid of the

Duke of Marlborough, to bring about the peace. The ministers devised the necessary intrigues. It was left to Swift to master and direct public opinion with the *Examiner* and with the pamphlets and lampoons with which he entertained, infuriated, aroused, and reassured the public.

The political situation was intricate in detail but simple in outline. King William, Prince of Orange, had involved his adoptive England with his native Holland in the Grand Alliance with Austria against France. There had for years been a war and there was still a war, of which some of the English were very tired. The victories of Marlborough abroad, though gratifying, were hardly as regular as the taxes at home. The landowners, who tended to be Tories, had begun to wonder whether they were not paying taxes to help the bankers and jobbers, who tended to be Whigs, reap enviable profits. Glory was something, but it cost money. Men muttered in country houses that the Duke had been riding his whirlwind a long time. They had noted that Godolphin, who as Lord Treasurer had furnished the war chest, was father to one of Marlborough's sons-in-law; and that Sunderland, Secretary of State, was a son-in-law himself. They had noted, also, that the Duchess, Mistress of the Robes and, it was said, mistress of Godolphin, did more than anybody else to make up the Queen's mind for her. Civil affairs, hardly less than military, were in the hands of Marlborough, who notoriously wanted to be Captain-General for life. A little more, and England would be mortgaged to the Marlboroughs.

Such a prospect ruffled and alarmed the Tories. Marlborough, veering like Godolphin with the Parliamentary wind, had formerly called himself a Tory, but now called himself a Whig. The Whigs must share the blame for the prolongation of the war, for the increase in taxes and prices. All that was insular in England resisted this burden laid upon it for the possible benefit of the Continent. The Whigs had been kind to the Dissenters to gain their support in Marlborough's enterprises. All that was orthodox in England resented this comfort given to the sects which threatened the unity and authority of the Church. Finding itself on the dizzy brink of altruism and liberalism, England had shrunk back in a passion for its good old virtues, its stout old order.

The change had not come of itself or from the disinterested conclusions of philosophers, but had been contrived and forwarded by Harley and St. John. Both of them had owed much to Marlborough, who in 1704 had approved of Harley for Secretary of State and of St. John for Secretary at War. Under the wings of that eagle they had plotted against his feathers. St. John had gifts of eloquence and manipulation which made him incomparable in the House of Commons. Harley, enough duller than his colleague to be more widely trusted, was adroit on the backstairs. Through his cousin Abigail Hill (Mrs. Masham), for whom the Duchess of Marlborough, also a cousin to the lady, had obtained a post in the Queen's bedchamber, his whispers reached his sovereign. Marlborough and Godolphin, becoming aware of a secret

influence against them, had in 1708 traced it to Harley
and had forced him out of the cabinet, along with
St. John. Harley had continued to whisper. The
Queen, resenting the constant pressure from the Duke
and Duchess, observing the popular unrest, and still
listening to the whispers, had been convinced that
the Whigs threatened the peace of the State and the
safety of the Church. From this had come the over-
throw of the Godolphin ministry and the sudden rise
to power of the Tories under the whispering Harley
and the glittering St. John. It was policy to win to
their side the wit whom they most desired to have with
them and most feared to have against them.

The arguments put forth may have been suggested
by any of the three men. Of the three, however, only
Swift can be credited with the high scorn, the grave
ingenuity of this polemic. It was he who, though he
thought Marlborough " as covetous as hell and ambitious as the prince of it," kept his friends from pressing
the Duke too hard. Swift had the tact to be content
with pointing out how much it was to the interest of
the commander-in-chief to have the war go on. Public
cynicism might be trusted to do the rest.

Nor did Swift use only arguments. He hit upon
the most insidious illustrations, such as his contrast
between the rewards of a Roman conqueror and those
of the Duke. British ingratitude, Swift figured out,
had already been worth something over half a million
pounds to the British general. Roman gratitude,
" which a victorious general received after his return
rom the most glorious expedition, conquered some

great kingdom, brought the king himself, his family, and nobles to adorn the triumph in chains, and made the kingdom either a Roman province or at best a poor depending state in humble alliance to that empire," would have amounted to less than a thousand pounds : incense, a sacrificial bull, an embroidered garment, a statue, a trophy, copper medals, a triumphal arch and car, and a laurel crown worth twopence.

Ingenious and insistent, Swift continued to pluck the same string until the public could hear no other note when it heard of Marlborough. After a year Marlborough fell, and the Duke of Ormond, whom Swift ranked next to Oxford (lately Harley) and Bolingbroke (lately St. John) among his friends, was put in command of the armies.

Towards the Whigs at large Swift turned an attention which was no less masterly. They were, for him, only a brawling faction, hungry for profits, and not more than a tenth of England. The Whigs, having made their fortunes at the expense of the majority, meant to go on making other fortunes, and would stop at no lying, no plotting, no uprising, no overthrowing which might serve their factious ends. At the same time, Swift would not admit that he was partisan. " We are unhappily divided into two parties," he said, " both which pretend a mighty zeal for our religion and government, only they disagree about the means. The evils we must fence against are, on one side, fanaticism and infidelity in religion, and anarchy, under the name of a commonwealth, in government ; on the other side, popery, slavery, and the Pretender from France." Between these two extremes of Whig and Tory Swift seemed to take his stand. Or rather, again, above both. He was still a clergyman, who put religion first among his concerns. He was not a politician, but the conscience of politicians. He was the conscience of England, tight in its island, deep in its prejudices, contemptuous of ideals and metaphysics, plain, sturdy, obstinate.

No position was so natural for Swift to take, as no position was so effective with the voters. Oxford and Bolingbroke might work out of sight with their intrigues. Swift never ceased to keep the eyes of the world upon their main purposes. British purposes, for the sake of British interests, through the exercise of British virtues. The Revolution was achieved. The Succession was established. It was time now to make peace with the Continent and to settle down to a British destiny. The change must not be too precipitate. Swift wrote as firmly against the ferocious Tories, demanding all places instantly for their party, as against the ousted Whigs. His variety was in his art, not in his argument. He could abuse, ridicule, hoax, lampoon, in grim prose or easy verse. He could parade the accomplishments of the Ministry in sober pamphlets or could raise clouds of bright dust to hoodwink the opposition. But always he was Swift, looking down from his peak at the whole race of mankind, only incidentally and temporarily supporting Oxford and Bolingbroke.

Throughout the Oxford administration Swift was

loyal, less out of need than out of love. When his associates, disregarding the Grand Alliance, made a stealthy treaty of peace with France ; when, insecure in the House of Lords, Oxford got the Queen to create a dozen Tory peers who would know why they were peers ; when England, at the Treaty of Utrecht, took the largest share of the spoils though she had tricked and abandoned the allies : even then Swift loved his friends. Passionately loyal, he could be affectionately blind.

In Oxford's thick skin Swift saw a stoic dignity, and in Oxford's procrastination something not too far from a noble patience. " Regular in life," Swift described the Lord Treasurer to the Archbishop of Dublin, " with a true sense of religion, an excellent scholar and a good divine, of a very mild and affable disposition, intrepid in his notions and indefatigable in business, an utter despiser of money for himself yet frugal, perhaps to an extremity, for the public." Nor about Boling-broke, libertine in thought and habit, would Swift be squeamish. He admired that " graceful, amiable person " and that mind " which was adorned with the choicest gifts that God hath yet thought fit to bestow upon the children of men." It was true that the Secretary had been " too great and criminal a pursuer " of pleasures which could " by no means be reconciled to religion or morals." But, Swift explained, " he was fond of mixing pleasure with business, and of being esteemed excellent at both ; upon which account he had a great respect for the characters of Alcibiades and Petronius." Could Socrates resist the charm of Alcibiades, or Seneca the charm of Petronius ?

Swift, moralist that he was, was little less susceptible to the dissolute Secretary than to the decorous Treasurer. His affection covered them with its flood. Bolingbroke hated Oxford, and Oxford suspected Bolingbroke. There was harmony between them only for a few months, if so long as that. Yet Swift, by nature so misanthropic, by experience so wary, set out with them in what he thought was a fellowship of love.

Though he learned better, he remained, to the end of his great episode, somewhat at the mercy of his love. It was, of course, the corollary of his hate. Hitherto alone with his pride in what seemed to him a prison, he had been able to hate all those whose neglect had kept him there. Such companions as Stella and Addison had been only alleviating visitors. But now half the circle of his enemies had turned friends, and had entreated him to help them. They had taken him, apparently, to their hearts. They had let him, apparently, into their minds. They had given him a tiger's share not only in the battle but in the command. Swift, all of whose emotions were profound, responded with emotions which were simple : gratitude, fidelity, delight in effort, ardent comradeship. He was so exultant at being delivered from his prison that he did not notice that he had been brought out to be harnessed.

Oxford and Bolingbroke must have smiled at his generous tribute to their virtues. Others did. When Swift wrote to Peterborough, then in Vienna, that the ministers seemed " heartily to love one another " and that they loved him too, Peterborough, who had been sent on an embassy to get him out of the way of the intriguing pair, sceptically wondered how Swift had come " to frame a system—in the times we live in—to govern the world by love." Oxford and Bolingbroke did not trouble themselves over the excess of Swift's affection, any more than they minded his arrogance. They were men of the stormy world, determined to get places and keep them. They worked for profit. If Swift worked for love or hate, that was his business. He was not, perhaps, as indispensable as the backstairs Mrs. Masham, but he could hurt the Whigs. They gave him all the room they could spare and applauded his blows.

Loving too much, Swift hated too much, as in his attack on the Earl of Wharton. " He is," Swift said, " without the sense of shame or glory as some men are without the sense of smelling ; and therefore a good name to him is no more than a precious ointment would be to those. . . .

" He seems to be but an ill dissembler and an ill liar, though they are the two talents he most practises and most values himself upon. The ends he has gained by lying appear to be more owing to the frequency than the art of them ; his lies being sometimes detected in an hour, often in a day, and always in a week. . . . He swears solemnly he loves and will serve you, and your back is no sooner turned but he tells those about him you are a dog and a rascal. He goes constantly to prayers in the forms of his place, and will talk bawdy and blasphemy at the chapel door. He is a Presbyterian in politics and an atheist in religion, but he chooses at present to whore with a Papist. In his

commerce with mankind his general rule is to endeavour imposing on their understandings, for which
he has but one receipt, a composition of lies and oaths ;
and this he applies indifferently to a freeholder of forty
shillings and a privy councillor, by which the honest
are often either deceived or amused ; and either way
he gains his point. . . . With a good natural understanding, a great fluency in speaking, and no ill taste
of wit, he is generally the worst companion in the
world ; his thoughts being wholly taken up between
vice and politics so that bawdy, profaneness, and
business fill up his whole conversation. . . . As some
vain young fellows, to make a gallantry appear of
consequence, will choose to venture their necks by
climbing up a wall or window at midnight to a common
wench, where they might as freely have gone at the door
and at noonday ; so his Excellency, either to keep
himself in practice or to advance the fame of his politics,
affects the most obscure, troublesome, and winding
paths, even in the commonest affairs, those which
would as well be brought about in the ordinary forms
or which would proceed of course whether he inter-
vened or no.

" He bears the gallantries of his lady with the indifference of a stoic, and thinks them well recompensed
by a return of children to support his family, without
the fatigues of being a father.

" He has three predominant passions which you will
seldom observe united in the same man, as arising
from different dispositions of mind, and naturally
thwarting each other ; these are love of power, love of

money, and love of pleasure. They ride him sometimes by turns and sometimes all together. . . . He
was never known to refuse or keep a promise. . . .
But here I desire to distinguish between a promise and
a bargain ; for he will be sure to keep the latter, when
he has had the fairest offer."

There was, Swift insisted, nothing personal in his
remarks. " Whoever were to describe the nature of a
serpent, a wolf, a crocodile, or a fox must be understood to do it for the sake of others, without any personal love or hatred of the animals themselves." Nor
would Wharton take it personally. " When these
papers are public 'tis odds but he will tell me, as he
once did upon a like occasion, that ' he is damnably
mauled,' and then with the easiest transition in the
world ask about the weather or time of the day." And
in fact, when Swift encountered Wharton at White's
chocolate house after the character was publlshed,
" Lord Wharton saw me at the door, and I saw him
but took no notice and was going away, but he came
through the crowd, called after me, and asked me how
I did."

This was, as Swift said, " not a humour put on to
serve a turn or keep a countenance, not arising from
the consciousness of his innocence or any grandeur of
mind, but the mere unaffected bent of his nature."
Yet few moralists could have carried themselves more
justly under such abuse. Wharton needed no philosophy in the circumstances. Experience was enough to
tell him that Swift, accusing him of so finished, so
universal a villainy, had blamed him for what was

remarkably near a virtue. The victim himself looked brilliant in this glare of wrath. Swift's hate, in its white-hot excess, had grown creative and had shaped a monster which had an insolent animal beauty along with its human vices.

But not all of Swift's victims had Wharton's whistling unconcern. There was the Duchess of Somerset, the red-haired Mistress of the Robes after the Marlboroughs had gone from Court. She had disliked Swift before he joined the Tories. With Lady Giffard, Temple's sister, she had resented the final volume of Temple's memoirs in 1709. It contained reflections on certain of the Whig lords, and Swift had published it. The Duchess, friend to Whigs, decided that he was " a man of no principle, either of honour or religion." Swift, knowing this, perversely circulated a lampoon in which he called her " Carrots " and brought up the old charge that she had connived in the assassination of her second husband. The Duchess, who though she had reached a third husband at fifteen had had no other for nearly thirty years, never forgave Swift. More than any of his enemies, more than the Archbishop of York, who inflexibly held the *Tale of a Tub* against him, she stood between him and the favour of the Queen. He might serve the ministers as only he could, but he could not become a bishop without the Queen's approval. That, while the angry Duchess lived, he could not get. And the Duchess outlived the Queen.

More love than he needed, more hate than he needed : these were what hampered Swift in politics.

translation of Homer into English verse, for which, he said, he must have them all subscribe. ' For,' says he, ' the author shall not begin to print till I have a thousand guineas for him.' Lord Treasurer, after leaving the Queen, came through the room, beckoning Dr. Swift to follow him. Both went off just before prayers."

Painful and shocking to see a genius so happy in his business, when it was such small business to be happy in. This was not the carriage of a man who, for all his sporadic arrogance, would force great rewards from his patrons.

Throughout 1711 and most of 1712 Swift worked too hard and too exultantly to have much time for hopes. He wrote often to Stella of his return to Ireland. Ormond might give him an addition to Laracor. He might get a Dublin parish. When Peterborough talked of bishops and deans Swift said his highest ambition was " to live in England, and with a competency to support me with honour." It was nearly enough to be able to advance his friends. The ministers declared that Swift never came to them without a Whig in his sleeve.

But by the third winter of his power he had begun to starve on his diet of promises. The rumour that he had been made Dean of Wells, when he had not, fretted him. The deaneries of Ely and Lichfield were vacant to no advantage of his. The Ministry must, he grumbled through the winter, do something for him or he would go back to Laracor. In January 1713 he wrote to Oxford : " I most humbly beg leave to inform your Lordship that the Dean of Wells died this morning at one o'clock. I entirely submit my poor fortunes to your Lordship." And Bolingbroke wrote to Swift with a rhythmic unction : " Though I have not seen you I did not fail to write to Lord Treasurer. *Non tua res agitur*, dear Jonathan. It is the Treasurer's cause ; it is my cause ; it is every man's cause who is embarked in our bottom. Depend upon it that I never will neglect any opportunity of showing that true esteem, that sincere affection and honest friendship for you which fill the breast of your faithful servant."

It was a ministerial vow. That same month the bishopric of Hereford was filled, but not by Swift. In April, when the Treaty of Utrecht had at last been signed and Swift considered his work done, there were vacant preferments on every tree : in England the deaneries of Wells, Ely, and Lichfield and the canonry of Windsor ; in Ireland the bishoprics of Raphoe and Dromore. Not one of them fell to Swift. Oxford shuffled. Bolingbroke had Swift to dinner. The Archbishop of York shook his head. The Duchess of Somerset hissed. The Queen held out. She would not have Swift a dean or canon in England, or a bishop anywhere. Help came from the Duke of Ormond. If the present Dean of St. Patrick's in Dublin might be made Bishop of Dromore, Swift could have that deanery. The Queen consented.

Oxford suddenly became eager to keep Swift in England. Let him be prebendary of Windsor. " Thus," wrote Swift, " he perplexes things. I expect neither. But I confess, as much as I love England, I am so angry at this treatment that if I had my choice I would rather have St. Patrick's." Did he remember that his old friend Robert Hunter, now governor of New York, had lately written that he wished Swift could come to be bishop there? No matter. The appointment was patched up, and Swift became, as he was to be for the rest of his life, the Dean of St. Patrick's.

"All that the Court or Ministry did for me was to let me choose my station in the country where I am banished." He was not even allowed to become Historiographer, to chronicle the reign which he no longer influenced.

This was the career and this the climax of Swift's life among the great. After a summer in Ireland he was, it is true, called back to London for the fourth and last winter of the Ministry, but his own future was settled, and his time was chiefly taken up with keeping the peace between Oxford and Bolingbroke. They were, it seemed to Swift, " a ship's crew quarrelling in a storm, or while their enemies are within gunshot." The fellowship of love had ceased to exist even for Swift's loyal eyes.

The victors were wrangling over the spoils. What about their futures? The Queen would not live for ever. The Elector of Hanover, upon whom the Succession had been fixed, was certain to be favourable to the Whigs. Both Oxford and Bolingbroke, both secretly, were dealing with the Pretender, willing to ruin the Succession if they could bring in a prince favourable to Tories. Meanwhile the mutinous Bolingbroke had determined to be first minister himself.

Out-intriguing Oxford, he won Oxford's cousin, now Lady Masham, to another allegiance. London and Windsor buzzed and rumbled. All winter and all spring Swift struggled to divert or pacify the wranglers. Their war went on. Swift, despairing, took to a dull, angry retreat in Berkshire. In July 1714 Oxford was forced to break the white staff of his office. Bolingbroke, however, did not supplant him. In five days the Queen died. The Whiggish Elector was to become George I. Marlborough, returning from the Continent, entered London with two hundred men on horseback, drums, and fifty coaches.

Swift, in a letter to Oxford, said farewell to such power as he had had. " In your public capacity," he told him, " you have often angered me to the heart, but as a private man, never once. . . . I will never write to you, if I can help it, otherwise than as to a private person, nor allow myself to have been obliged by you in any other capacity. The memory of one great instance of your candour and justice I will carry to my grave : that having been in a manner domestic with you for almost four years, it was never in the power of any public or concealed enemy to make you think ill of me, though malice and envy were often employed to that end. If I live, posterity shall know that and more, which . . . is all the return I can make you. Will you give me leave to say how I would desire to stand in your memory : as one who was truly sensible of the honour you did him, though he was too proud to be vain upon it ; as one who was neither assuming, officious, nor teasing, who never wilfully misrepresented persons or facts to you, nor consulted his passions when he gave a character ; and lastly, as one whose indiscretions proceeded altogether from a weak head, and not an ill heart ? I will add one thing more, which is the highest compliment I can make : that I was never afraid of offending you, nor am I now in any pain for the manner I write to you in. I have said enough ; and, like one at your levee, having made my bow, I shrink back into the crowd."

3

Hardly had Swift reached London in 1710 when he sat four hours one morning to the fashionable Charles Jervas, who, having begun a portrait on Swift's previous visit to England, now gave the picture " quite another turn." Perhaps he put the gleam of higher prospects into those eyes which in their extreme moods ranged from fire to stone. Full-lidded, bold even under the dark and heavy brows, humorously but not secretively averted, they seemed in the portrait to glance at something and to stare at everything. Swift's periwig did not conceal his proud, arched forehead. His clerical bands plumped out his well-nourished, worldly chin, double and dimpled. His nose was both inquiring and commanding, ready to be contemptuous at the first excuse. But about his mouth there were the signs of another nature, sensitive, nervous, never calm. The corners would twitch easily, the lips tremble : the lower disciplined to a counterfeit of straightness, but the upper, short and friendly, indisciplinably sweet.

This was the face of a man whom nothing on earth could over-awe, yet who would assert himself too much out of mere touchiness. He would frighten others yet would hold them, fascinated, dangerously near him. He would give and receive much love and little happiness. This was the face that was to be among the best known in London for four years, this stout body somewhat taller than most men's, this mind more restless than any man's.

The Jervas portrait was but the notation of a few hours. The true likeness of Swift in his days of power he drew himself, in the journal-letters to Stella which he posted whenever his sheet of paper was full. Before he left his bed in the morning, after he got into it at night, at any time during the day, Swift set down, with minor interruptions, a continuous account of all, or almost all, he did. He took it for granted that Stella was interested in whatever concerned him. His journal was partly news sent from the great world to a friend waiting in a small one, but it was partly, also, a detailed memorandum written as for his other self. He could be confiding, indiscreet, coarse, boastful, hilarious, tender, admonitory, savage, absurd, pouring out what came to him as it came. He wrote now as if this were a letter to Stella and Rebecca Dingley both, or to either of them ; now as if it were a conversation with himself, in the knowledge that they, and only they, would hear.

The journal was so intimate that he fell often into a foolish " little language," like a giant talking to a baby with what he imagined was the baby's vocabulary and pronunciation—or like a lover using silly words in despair of finding any that were serious enough. Swift's baby-talk was a joke kept up between him and Stella, a note of tenderness struck in this way for want of a chance to sound it with a voice. But he did not talk down to her. He told her his life.

"I was this morning at ten at the rehearsal of Mr. Addison's play, called *Cato*, which is to be acted on Friday. There were not above half-a-score of us to see it. We stood on the stage, and it was foolish enough to see the actors prompted every moment, and the poet directing them ; and the drab that acts Cato's daughter out in the midst of a passionate part and then calling out 'What's next ?' The Bishop of Clogher was there too, but he stood privately in a gallery. I went to dine with Lord Treasurer, but he was gone to Wimbledon, his daughter Carmarthen's country seat, seven miles off. So I went back and dined privately with Mr. Addison, whom I had left to go to Lord Treasurer. I keep fires yet ; I am very extravagant. I sat this evening with Sir Andrew Fountaine. . . . It is rainy weather again ; nevle saw ze rike [never saw the like]. This letter shall go to-morrow. Remember, ung oomens, it is seven weeks since your last, and I allow oo but five weeks. But oo have been galloping in the country."

The variety of Swift's days was in the persons he met and talked with. His habits had the regularity which goes with being virtuous and poor. He made, however, no virtue of his poverty. "I love these shabby difficulties when they are over ; but I hate them, because they arise from not having a thousand pounds a year."

Though he liked best to make his own meal of a single dish, he despised a skimpy table. Though he liked to walk, and took a chair or coach only in bad weather, he minded the expense when he had to ride, not his loss of an opportunity to trudge like a hero. He thought he was extravagant about fires, but when he shivered in his lodgings it was because coal cost money, not because shivering exalted his spirit. He avoided fruit, he more or less gave up snuff, he put water in his wine. All these asceticisms were for the sake of his treacherous health, as was the brandy that he drank, as were the pills and purges, the drops and ointments with which he fought his many attacks of giddiness. But never once did he rejoice in the endurance of a saint or the glory of a martyr. He did not relish even the fasts of his Church. " I hate Lent. I hate different diets, and furmity and butter, and herb porridge, and sour devout faces of people who only put on religion for seven weeks."

Swift was a man of his world in his frank admiration for power, station, wealth, comfort, elegance, urbanity, learning, wit, manners. He had come to England to seek a better society than there was in Laracor or Dublin. His natural handicaps—passion, intensity, genius—were enough. He would not pretend that his lack of fortune was a merit. He complained of it, desired to mend it, and kept the best company he could.

Each morning in his various London lodgings

Patrick, the servant whom Swift had brought over from Ireland, woke his master early, not always the first time he called. Swift's sleep was heavy but disturbed. " I was dreaming the most melancholy things of poor Ppt [Poppet], and was grieving and crying all night." Awake, he was likely to stay in bed till the room was warm, writing, often still by candlelight, as if Stella and Dingley were beside him. " Morning. I am going this morning to see Prior, who dines with me at Mr. Harley's ; so I can't stay fiddling and talking with dear little brats in a morning, and 'tis terribly cold. I wish my cold hand was in the warmest place about you, young women. I'd give ten guineas upon that account with all my heart, faith. Oh, it starves my thigh. So I'll rise and bid you good morrow, my ladies both, good morrow. Come, stand away, let me rise. Patrick, take away the candle. Is there a good fire ? So—up adazy."

Shaving, every second or third day ; brandy, on days when he was giddy ; breakfast of milk porridge or a cake Stella's mother had made him : these got Swift ready for his day. He might write at home, all day when he was busiest, sending out for a chop and a pot of ale for his dinner. But usually he put on periwig, boots, and black gown with pudding-sleeves, and left the house, walking, about his pleasure or his affairs. Perhaps he had morning tea or chocolate with some of the ladies who delighted in his fame and insolence. Perhaps he conferred with his printers in the City. Perhaps he waited on one of the lords of his political fellowship. There were many amusements in London.

"Lady Kerry, Mrs. Pratt, Mrs. Cadogan, and I in one coach, Lady Kerry's son and his governor and two gentlemen in another, maids and misses and little master (Lord Shelburne's children) in a third, all hackneys, set out at ten o'clock this morning from Lord Shelburne's house in Piccadilly to the Tower, and saw all the sights, lions, etc., then to Bedlam ; then dined at the chop-house behind the Exchange ; then to Gresham College (but the keeper was not at home) ; and concluded the night at the puppet-show, whence we came home safe at eight."

The pivot of Swift's day was dinner, usually at three. First with Whigs, then with Tories, he dined through the town and out of it. "That's something charms me mightily about London, that you go dine a dozen miles off in October, stay all day, and return so quickly. You cannot do anything like this in Dublin." Within a month after the Whigs clutched at him he had more invitations than he had afternoons. He was a wit and scholar ; he was a man of influence with the Ministry. Noblemen with axes to grind begged him to come to their tables. Men less interested in his power no less eagerly took up the fashion. Obliging hosts urged him to make his own terms.

"I dined to-day with a lady of my acquaintance, who was sick, in her bedchamber, upon three herrings and a chicken ; the dinner was my bespeaking." "Dr. Arbuthnot . . . yesterday gave me my choice of place, persons, and victuals for to-day. So I chose to dine with Mrs. Hill . . . Mrs. Masham's sister ; no company but us three, and to have a shoulder of mutton, a small one ; which was exactly, only there was too much victuals besides, and the Doctor's wife was of the company." Nor did Swift make terms only with friends of his own level. Bolingbroke " showed me his bill of fare to tempt me to dine with him. Poh, said I, I value not your bill of fare. Give me your bill of company." About both the food and the other diners Swift was firm. At the Earl of Abingdon's " we had nothing but fish. . . . Our wine was poison. . . . His carps were raw, and his candles tallow. He shall not catch me in haste again." And again : " I left a friend's house to-day where I was invited, just when dinner was setting on, and pretended I was engaged, because I saw some fellows I did not know."

Better a slice of mutton in his lodgings than indifferent or too numerous dishes ; better his own company than that of " persons unknown, as bad, for aught I know, as your deans, parsons, and curates." Swift rode high, and all Tory London encouraged him.

At many houses where he dined the guests stayed on for the evening. Swift chose generally to leave at six, to walk in Hyde Park, to visit other friends, to sit in a coffee-house—though after a few months of his influence with Oxford he gave up coffee-houses as too public. Many of his evenings he went home to write, at first an occasional *Tatler*, then his weekly *Examiner*, afterwards his pamphlets, at any time his stinging verses. In his lodgings he might find that Patrick had forgotten the fire or had neglected to buy coal or had gone off with the key with which Swift's papers were locked up. There would be abuse and apology, neither of which meant anything. The most regular interruptions of Swift's evenings came from Oxford, who kept " cursed hours," sometimes did not dine till five, and liked Swift to be with him at supper. " I hate these suppers mortally, but I seldom eat anything." Such evenings with Oxford were likely to be long and convivial, and wearing to Swift, who drank little, ate less, liked as well to sit beside card-players as to play himself, and was soon bored by ordinary conversation.

Yet when he had reached his bed and had put on his nightgown and velvet nightcap—the fur-trimmed one which Dingley sent was " too little and too hot "— he remembered, no matter how late it was, the journal. " Pshaw, I must be writing to those dear saucy brats every night, whether I will or no, let me have what business I will, or come home ever so late, or be ever so sleepy ; but an old saying and a true one,

> " ' *Be you lords or be you earls,*
> *You must write to naughty girls.*' "

Widely as Swift dined, three days a week were for much of the year given to his special friends. On Sunday, after going to Court, which he said served him " as a coffee-house," he usually dined with Bolingbroke. " Mr. Secretary had too much company with him to-day ; so I came away soon after dinner. I give no man liberty to swear or talk bawdy, and I found some of them were in constraint, so I left them to themselves." On Saturday Swift dined with Oxford for what the first minister called his " whipping day " —the day, that is, when the informal cabinet reviewed the past week and designed the next. "This company at first consisted only of the Lord Keeper Harcourt, the Earl Rivers, the Earl of Peterborough, Mr. Secretary St. John, and myself ; and here, after dinner, they used to discourse and settle matters of great importance. Several lords were afterwards, by degrees, admitted. . . . These meetings were always continued except when the Queen was at Windsor ; but, as they grew more numerous, became of less consequence, and ended only in drinking and general conversation." The matters of great importance were the Ministry's policies and intrigues. The general conversation has been lost.

Swift told Stella only that he and his friends had talked, seldom what they had said. Once, not on a Saturday, when he had opposed the appointment of a certain commissioner to Spain because he was a " most covetous cur," Swift reported the argument with Oxford. " I went on and said it was a shame to send him ; to which he agreed, but desired I would name some who understood business and do not love money, for he could not find them. I said there was something in a treasurer different from other men ; that we ought not to make a man a bishop who does not love divinity, or a general who does not love war ; and I wondered why the Queen would make a man lord treasurer who does not love money. . . . Is it not silly to write all this ? But it gives you an idea what our conversation is with mixed company." When the Earl of Nottingham had deserted to the Whig side " Lord Treasurer was hinting as if he wished a ballad was made on him, and

I will get up one against to-morrow. . . . I was this morning making the ballad, two degrees above Grub Street . . . and then went to dine with our Society. . . . The printer came before we parted, and brought the ballad, which made them laugh very heartily a dozen times."

The Society which laughed at the ballad claimed the third fixed dinner of Swift's week, Thursday, though only during the session of Parliament. Bolingbroke seems to have planned the club in June 1711, when Swift was in the country with Lord Shelburne. It was to be small, weighty, and decent, without the extravagance of the Kit-Cat or the drunkenness of the Beef-Steak, was to be made up of men of wit and men of influence, and was to have for its two great ends " the improvement of friendship and the encouragement of letters." Swift, back in town, found himself among the original twelve members and at once the eagerest. " If we go on as we begin," he wrote to Stella, "no other club in this town will be worth talking of." The men of wit were Swift, Prior, and John Arbuthnot, the Queen's physician. There were three times as many men of influence. Oxford and Harcourt were excluded, since the club meant to appeal to them for patronage. But their sons were chosen, and Oxford's son-in-law, Viscount Dupplin, and Samuel Masham, the husband of Oxford's whispering cousin. There were, also, Bolingbroke, Sir Robert Raymond, Solicitor-General, Allen Bathurst, George Granville, Secretary at War, and Sir William Wyndham.

The members, putting off their titles when they dined, called each other " Brother." Each in turn was president of the dinner and paid the bill until all had had turns, after which the charges of each dinner were divided among them. They dined sometimes at the houses of the members, more often at taverns. The dozen or so brothers added after the first twelve were all on the side of influence rather than of wit. The richer members, who were men of influence, ran up the cost of their dinners so that the poorer, who were men of wit, could not afford it. Yet Swift, though he winced at his bill for seven guineas, for a year and a half was happy. Power and learning had sat down in an equal brotherhood. When the Duke of Ormond brought his brother the Earl of Arran, who was not a member, to a meeting against all order, Swift opposed his election to the face of the Earl and the Duke. But Swift was exultant when four of his brothers were among the twelve peers whom Oxford packed into the House of Lords : the son-in-law Dupplin, the cousin-in-law Masham, Bathurst, and Granville.

It took Swift a year and a half to realize how much more skill than he the men of influence had at getting what they wanted. Having odd wells of enthusiasm in him, he had imagined that a club of politicians could be as much interested in the encouragement of letters as in the improvement of friendship.

The day after the first meeting in June 1711 he urged Oxford to leave Congreve, though a Whig, in his post. Oxford said he would. Swift hurried off to Congreve with the news. " So I have made a worthy man happy, and that is a good day's work." And Swift that same day had larger plans. " I am proposing to my Lord to erect a society or academy for correcting and settling our language, that we may not perpetually be changing as we do. He enters mightily into it." The pamphlet on " correcting, ascertaining, and improving the English tongue " was the only piece of writing Swift ever published with his name. He wrote again like a governor, demanding that the language be orderly and stable, regulated by a lawful academy. He wrote, no less, like a brother of the Society, appealing to Oxford to become the patron of worthy, needy men of letters. Nothing came of these proposals, though Oxford brimmed with promises.

Swift undertook to raise money among the members. In February 1713 he had collected sixty guineas and was " to give them away to two authors to-morrow; and Lord Treasurer has promised us a hundred pounds to reward some others." The sixty pounds went to the two authors, but there was another in worse need. That was " little Harrison," a young Oxford poet for whom Swift had one of his profound, inexplicable tendernesses. " I went in the morning, and found him mighty ill, and got . . . an order for a hundred pounds from the Treasury to be paid him to-morrow ; and I have got him removed to Knightsbridge for air." The next day : " I . . . desired a friend to receive the hundred pounds for poor Harrison, and will carry it to him to-morrow morning." The day after that : " I took Parnell this morning, and we walked to see poor Harrison. I had the hundred pounds in my pocket. I told Parnell I was afraid to knock at the door ; my mind misgave me. I knocked, and his man in tears told me his master was dead an hour before. . . . Lord Treasurer was much concerned when I told him. I could not dine with Lord Treasurer nor anywhere else, but got a bit of meat toward evening."

This pathetic episode, hardly more than a touch of melodrama in the general drama of Swift's venture, cut him more sharply than his own mounting disappointment. He had thought that though he might not help himself he might at least help others. Now it seemed he could not do even that. He had only kept a few Whig poets in their places. His scheme for an academy which was to honour and establish letters among the English was still a mere scheme somewhere on the wind. The Ministry which he had served was not, after all, to be renowned for its patronage to learning. The man of wit had looked vainly to the men of influence.

What Swift, whose pride played tricks with his vision, did not see was that he had exploited his wit much as Oxford had exploited all the wit at his command. Oxford had used such men of letters as could be bent to his political concerns. Swift had bent his talents to pamphlets and lampoons about the most temporary matters. From Prior he had learned to write verse more lightly as from Addison he had learned to write more smoothly. Swift had poured his tremendous prose on the ground, careless what became of it. Obsessed with the desire for power, he had tried to win it by such force as politicians use, not by the art natural to him ; among his pretended brothers the Dupplins and Mashams, not among his true friends, the Arbuthnots and Popes.

4

During his final winter in England Swift turned to his true friends. It was not because he had found where he belonged. It was because he knew he had failed to belong elsewhere. He was not a bishop. He was not even an English dean. He was only a great writer, author of a great satire, making his first plans for the greatest of satires, meditating a revenge. But his revenge hardly went, that year, beyond a prospectus. He and Arbuthnot had taken up the rising young poets Parnell, Gay, and Pope. All five met Saturday evenings at Arbuthnot's rooms in St. James's Palace, where the Scriblerus Club, as they called themselves, plotted a burlesque biography which was to ridicule false learning.

Oxford had called Swift Dr. Martin, " because martin is a sort of a swallow, and so is a swift." From that had come the name of Martinus Scriblerus, a phantom pedant whose career the Club was to trace through all his foolish blunders. The leader seems to have been Arbuthnot. " To talk of Martin in any hands but yours," Swift wrote to him, " is a folly. You every day give better hints than all of us together could do in a twelvemonth. . . . Pope, who first thought of the hint, has no genius at all to it, in my mind. Gay is too young. Parnell has some ideas of it, but is idle. I could put together, and lard, and strike out well enough. But all that relates to the sciences must be from you." Arbuthnot wrote the history of Martin's youth and education so wittily that Sterne later pilfered from it for his history of Tristram Shandy. Pope, hunting among contemporary poets for examples of bathos, " the art of sinking in poetry," took the first steps in his war upon the dunces. Swift was to exhibit Martin on his travels, and had already thought of taking him among pigmies, among giants, among fantastic scientists.

The break in the Ministry and the death of the Queen scattered the Scriblerus Club. Though the members often spoke of it in their letters, the treatise remained fragments. " I must be a little easy in my mind before I can think of Scriblerus," Swift wrote to Pope. It was not merely an uneasy mind which kept Swift from going on with the project. Whether or not he was yet aware of it, the scheme was too small for him. He could no longer be content, as he might have been in the days of the *Tale of a Tub*, to ridicule pedants.

Swift certainly was not aware, at the Saturday meetings of the Club, that his friends had by nature a better art than he could ever learn : the art of valuing their best gifts most, the art of being satisfied to be themselves. What he did with them he thought of as play. His work, he thought, was his efforts, vain as they were, in behalf of Oxford and Bolingbroke. He stood between the ministers and the poets, eager to be generous. " Of all the world," Pope wrote, " you are the man, without flattery, who serve your friends with the least ostentation. It is almost ingratitude to thank you, considering your temper." Swift introduced Parnell to the ministers and interested Bolingbroke in Parnell's poetry. Swift helped Gay to his post as secretary with the envoy to Hanover. Swift got for Pope's translation of Homer such a list of subscribers as no book had ever had in England. Swift struck the vein which in Arbuthnot " lay like a mine in the earth, which the owner for a long time never knew of." But Swift did not take a benefit from their examples.

How could he ? Parnell was humble and drifting. Gay was sensual and lazy, ready to be any man's dependent, troubled only because patrons were too few. Pope was first and last a poet who schemed, fought, and lived for his art, as Swift for action. Arbuthnot was a man of learning and judgment, of whom Swift said that he had " more wit than we all have " and Pope said that in wit and humour he was " superior to all mankind " ; but Arbuthnot was not ambitious or misanthropic. He might scorn the world, but he amply took it as it came. Of all the patterns by which these others shaped their lives, not a single pattern fitted Swift.

When, after a summer spent in dejected, furious retirement at Letcombe in Berkshire, writing various apologias for the fallen Ministry, Swift went back to Ireland in September 1714, he was beaten but not reconciled. His impulse was still towards the central fountains of honour and profit and power. His obsessive desire to master and direct had not, after all his disappointments, left him in even a sullen peace. Having been beaten, and not reconciled, he could not study his failure in a clear light. He did not understand that with his gifts, wit and learning, passion and intensity and genius, he had been at a disadvantage with men who had wealth and office, and that though he could pass them in the long run, he could not be immediately equal with them. The fault, as he explained it to himself, did not lie in his passion to do what he was not chiefly designed to do, nor in the incompetence and deviousness of his political associates, nor in the catastrophe of the Queen's death. It lay, he somehow concluded, in the very constitution of human life.

Let virtue work and sweat as it would to bring order out of the dirty chaos, nothing permanent could come of it. For a time a few resolute men might hold up the dreadful weight with their shoulders. But if there should be one tremor, the momentary pattern would collapse and the parts of it return to their obstinate disorder. There was no hope. Scorn and hate were all that any virtuous or reasonable man could feel towards mankind.

I

JEERS followed Swift out of England, and jeers greeted him in Ireland. Dublin was full of Whigs. Laracor, which he had kept along with his deanery, was desolate. " I would retire too, if I could," he wrote after a month to Bolingbroke, " but my country seat, where I have an acre of ground, is gone to ruin. The wall of my own apartment is fallen down, and I want mud to rebuild it and straw to thatch it. Besides, a spiteful neighbour has seized on six feet of ground, carried off my trees, and spoiled my grove. . . . I have not fortitude enough to go and see those devastations. But, in return, I live a country life in town, see nobody, and go every day once to prayers ; and hope, in a few months, to grow as stupid as the present situation of affairs will require. Well, after all, parsons are not such bad company, especially when they are under subjection ; and I let none but such come near me." So a banished general might have said it was not so bad to spend his time drilling a squad of militia in a distant province.

" You are to understand," Swift wrote after ten months to Pope, " that I live in the corner of a vast unfurnished house. My family consists of a steward, a groom, a helper in the stables, a footman, and an old maid who are all at board wages, and when I do not dine abroad or make an entertainment, which last is very rare, I eat a mutton pie and drink half a pint of wine. My amusements are defending my small dominions against the archbishop and endeavouring to reduce my rebellious choir." So a deposed prime minister might have turned his hand to the government of a village.

Swift did not neglect his chores. He set to work to subdue the " three and twenty dignitaries and prebendaries " who made up his chapter as St. Patrick's. The chapter yielded. He began to resist his superiors, particularly the bishops who had deprived him of credit for the grant of the First Fruits. The bishops became wary. Even in Laracor, where Swift was only vicar, he demanded better manners from the Welsh bishop of the diocese, and, somewhat later, wrote to him as vicars seldom write to bishops : " I am only sorry that you, who are of a country famed for good nature, have found a way to unite the hasty passion of your own countrymen with the long, sedate resentment of a Spaniard ; but I have an honourable hope that this proceeding has been more owing to party than complexion." Though Swift refused for half a dozen years to mix in the business of the world which had defeated him, he was, from the first, gigantic and ominous in his exile.

There was need of caution. During his stay in England he had got out of touch with Irish affairs, as well as out of sympathy. London had run him into debt. As dean and vicar he was to have about six or seven hundred pounds a year when he could get them : an income which made him, he said, the poorest man in Ireland who dined off plate and the richest who did not drive his carriage. But the installation at St. Patrick's cost a thousand pounds and several stringent years. The Whigs suspected Swift, like the late ministers, of disloyalty to George I. The suspicion was absurd. " I look upon the coming of the Pretender," Swift said, " as a greater evil than any we are likely to suffer under the worst Whig ministry that can be found." Yet when Oxford, Bolingbroke, and Ormond —" three persons from among the rest of mankind on whose friendship and protection I might depend, whose conversation I most valued and chiefly confined myself to "—were charged with the treason of plotting to bring the Pretender in, when Ormond and Bolingbroke escaped to France and Oxford went to the Tower, Swift shared their odium.

The authorities, intercepting letters sent to him, had a chance to read nothing more treasonable than these words to Ormond : " We have no new favourite, nor never can. You have left so sweet a relish by your conversation upon all our pleasures that we cannot bear the thoughts of intimacy with any person." With the wives of Bolingbroke and Ormond Swift carried on a guarded correspondence. To Oxford, in the Tower, he wrote without reserve, making him " the humblest offers of my poor service and attendance "—attendance, that is, in prison if Oxford would permit it. " It is the first time I ever solicited you in my own behalf, and if I am refused I think it will be the first request you ever refused me. I do not conceive myself obliged to regulate my opinions by the proceedings of a House of Lords or Commons ; and therefore, however they may acquit themselves in your Lordship's case, I shall take the liberty of thinking and calling you the ablest and faithfulest minister, the truest lover of your country, that this age hath produced." Oxford's son kept the letter "as a family monument." Oxford himself acknowledged it two years later.

While the Jacobite odium hung over Swift he declared, not quite in earnest, that he would hide himself away in Guernsey or Wales for the rest of his life. The world was too hateful to live in. Yet what most distressed him was his grief over the friends with whom he could no longer be "familiar and customary." "When I leave a country without a probability of returning," he wrote to Pope, "I think as seldom as I can of what I loved or esteemed in it, to avoid the *desiderium* which of all things makes life most uneasy." And to Arbuthnot he wrote : "Writing to you would make me stark mad. Judge his condition who has nothing to keep him from being miserable but endeavouring to forget those for whom he has the greatest value, love, and friendship."

His friends would not let him sink into such a gulf. "Never," Arbuthnot answered him, "repeat that melancholy, tender word, that you will endeavour to forget me. I am sure I never can forget you till I meet with, what is impossible, another whose conversation

I can delight so much in as Dr. Swift's. . . . That hearty, sincere friendship, that plain and open ingenuity in all your commerce, is what I am sure I can never find in another man. I shall want often a faithful monitor, one that would vindicate me behind my back and tell me my faults to my face." Pope wrote to him of " the constant esteem and affection I am both obliged and inclined to have for you," and said he regarded him " as a friend in another world," much as he regarded his patron saint. Bolingbroke wrote that for a half-hour's conversation with Swift he would " barter whole hours of life." For a year or more Swift could hardly bring himself to reply. Then, however, the rigour of his despair began to leave him, his wit to come out of the lair where it had sulked.

To Pope, in 1716, Swift pointed out the use of fools, who, in his opinion, were " as necessary for a good writer as pen, ink, and paper." He could take enough interest in wit to propose to Gay the subject of another pastoral. " What think you of a Newgate pastoral, among the whores and thieves there ? " In 1717 he wrote once more to Addison, now Secretary of State, congratulating Addison upon his post and the Whigs for having chosen one man on his merits. In 1718 Swift wrote to Oxford's son that time had sweetened him. " My servants tell all our neighbourhood that I grow gentler every day, and am content only to call my footman a fool for that which when you knew me first I would have broke his head." And in December 1719 Swift wrote to Bolingbroke a letter in which his humour played again over his passion.

" I can now express in a hundred words what would formerly have cost me ten. I can write epigrams of fifty distichs which might be squeezed into one. I have gone the round of all my stories three or four times with the younger people, and begin them again. I give hints how significant a person I have been, and nobody believes me. I pretend to pity them, but am inwardly angry. . . . If I boast of having been valued three hundred miles off, it is of no more use than if I told how handsome I was when I was young. . . . If I can prevail on any one to personate a hearer and admirer, you would wonder what a favourite he grows. He is sure to have the first glass out of the bottle and the best bit I can carve. Nothing has convinced me so much that I am of a little subaltern spirit, *inopis atque pusilli animi,* as to reflect how I am forced into the most trifling amusements to divert the vexation of former thoughts and present objects."

In another man this might have sounded like humility. In Swift it has, somehow, the imagined sound of a searchlight falling into a dark corner.

He was now almost Swift again. Looking back over his career as a wit he wrote an ironic letter of advice to a young poet, assuring him that poetry did not demand religion or learning or even sense of those who practised it. Ireland, he argued, must have a Grub Street. Ireland must have a poet laureate, a professor of poetry, a city bard for Dublin, a poet in fee for every parish. It might have more. " What if everyone so qualified were obliged to add one more than usual to the number of his domestics, and besides a fool and a chaplain (which are often united in one person) would retain a poet in his family ? " Looking back over his career as a parson Swift wrote a sober letter of advice to a young clergyman. To him, not to the poet, Swift said that " proper words in proper places make the true definition of a style."

Both these letters dealt with what for Swift was play. He resumed his work in a pamphlet urging all the Irish, as a protest against the ruinous export laws, to make a " universal use of Irish manufacture," " utterly rejecting and renouncing everything wearable that comes from England." Officials fumed. He was, they claimed, trying to divide the two kingdoms. The printer was brought to trial. When the jury acquitted him the Lord Chief Justice sent them back nine times, till they were willing to leave the verdict to the mercy of the judge. Though the case was dropped when the next Lord-Lieutenant came over, the damage was done. Swift, having once more tasted Whig blood, was on his way to becoming an Irish patriot.

2

But before he gathered all his forces he had to go through his final conflict with Stella's rival. The drama reaching its climax was already much too long.

He had met Vanessa (Esther Vanhomrigh) early in 1708 in London, where her mother was living with her children. It pleased the mother to call the daughter younger than she was, and it did not displease the daughter. She was a sleepy girl, still, at twenty, undecided between the nursery and the drawing-room, moody, idle, intelligent. Swift, at first considering her a child, discovered in her a mind, and was irresistibly, humorously impelled to shape it. "She had good principles," he wrote three years later, "and I have corrected all her faults." She had, however, the passion of sleepy women, not the obedience of Stella.

To that passion Swift was blind, first carelessly, then deliberately. No doubt he felt it. He had put his entire energy into his pride. His senses, no matter how cold towards women, must have learned that the relationship with Stella, no matter how close and kind, was sometimes dry and mild. She was nearly a wife, and some routine had got into their companionship. Vanessa was younger. Vanessa was new. Swift, for all his prudence, enjoyed the tumult in her disposition. Because he held her, as he seems always to have done, at a safe arm's-length, he was obtuse to her eagerness. Obtuse and insufficiently concerned. Being forty, he could not quite resist such warmth from a girl, did not have quite the courage to put out such a fire or leave it. Too scrupulous or too temperate to make the full use of Vanessa's passion, he went on idling within its perilous range. He was surprised when he found that he had on his hands a mistress as extraordinary as the wife he had in Ireland.

Stella the extraordinary wife. Vanessa the extraordinary mistress. Swift the extraordinary husband and lover. No other terms will bound the extraordinary triangle. Gossip then and gossip since has wasted its strength in trying to find out whether Swift was

technically lover or husband to either of the women.
What if he was ? What if he was not ? The drama
remains the same.

Stella was for nearly forty years, child and woman,
" the truest, most virtuous and valuable friend that
I," Swift said, " or perhaps any other person, ever was
blessed with." Call Stella his wife or be pedantic.
Vanessa was for fifteen years his occasional companion,
his delight, his torment, to whom he wrote—in bad
French—that there was no merit nor any proof of his
good taste in his finding in her all that nature had
given any mortal in the way of honour, virtue, sense,
wit, tenderness, agreeableness, and firmness of spirit.
Call Vanessa his mistress or be pedantic. One side of
Swift looked towards a wife, one towards a mistress.
He maintained between them a singular course, but it
was no more singular than his character. He was, after
all, only one man loved by two women.

The friendship begun in 1708 between Swift and
Vanessa, anxious to be possessed but willing to be
taught, was kept up during that stay in England and,
by letters, during his next absence in Ireland. When
he returned to become a Tory in 1710 he had so lavish
a welcome from the Vanhomrighs that their house
became almost his. He lived near them, dined with
them often and then more often, and had a small room
there in which to read and write.

Stella, hearing about them, seems to have sniffed.
" You say they are of no consequence," he answered
her. " Why, they keep as good female company as I
do male. I see all the drabs of quality at this end of

Esther Vanhomrigh (Vanessa)

the town with them." He spoke in his journal rather
of the mother or of the whole family than of Vanessa.

When, having taken to Chelsea in the spring of
1711, he walked more or less daily to London and back,
he kept his best gown and periwig at the Vanhomrigh house, and called twice a day to change. Vanessa,
with the family, possibly visited him in Chelsea, as she
probably did at Kensington in the summer of the
year after. The Vanhomrighs certainly visited Swift
at Windsor in September 1712, and Vanessa was on
some score disappointed. " Why then," he wrote,
" you should not have come, and I knew that as well
as you."

So far any strong feelings there may have been in
either of them had not risen into words. He teased her
for her dawdling, for her chiding, for her jealousy of
her younger sister, for her habit of coaxing him for
political secrets. She complained, rather childishly, of
his neglect of her when he was out of London. Their
letters might have been between Swift and any young
woman of his acquaintance.

But when he went to Ireland in June 1713, sick of
England, Vanessa could not endure the stern break
which suited him. The four letters she wrote before
she got an answer were disconsolate. " I find no conversation on earth comparable but yours." She had
heard of his illness. " Oh ! what would I give to know
how you do at this instant. My fortune is too hard.
Your absence was enough, without this cruel addition."
" How could you be so cruel, to defer telling me
the thing of the world I wished most to know ? If you

think I write too much, your only way is to tell me so, or at least to write to me again, that I may know you don't quite forget me ; for I very much fear that I never employ a thought of yours now, except when you are reading my letters, which makes me ply you with them. . . . If you are very happy it is ill-natured of you not to tell me, except 'tis what is inconsistent with mine."

Swift could not mistake this last clause. In seven words Vanessa made plain that she was wondering whether he could be happy without her, asking whether he was by any dreadful chance happy with someone else, announcing that she thought of him and her as having their happiness in common. His answer put cold oceans between them.

" I had your last spleenatic letter. I told you when I left England I would endeavour to forget everything there, and would write as seldom as I could. I did indeed design one general round of letters to my friends, but my health has not yet suffered me. I design to pass the greatest part of the time I stay in Ireland here in the cabin where I am now writing ; neither will I leave the kingdom till I am called for ; and if they have no further service for me I will never see England again. At my first coming I thought I should have died with discontent, and was horribly melancholy while they were installing me. But it begins to wear off and change to dulness. My river walk is extremely pretty, and my canal in great beauty, and I see trouts playing in it."

Her ardour, that is, he saw as spleen. He meant to

forget her along with all the others. If he were to go back it would be to politics. He was dull but not melancholy. Vanessa would be glad to know that there were fish in his canal.

Politics called Swift back in September to London and to Vanessa. There are no letters belonging to that winter, but there is the poem, apparently written then, in which Swift told the story of Cadenus (that is *Decanus*, dean) and Vanessa.

He began lightly, with the graces of a contemporary wit. The shepherds and the nymphs, he said, had gone to law before the court of Venus, the nymphs accusing the shepherds of resisting love, the shepherds defending themselves by the counter-accusation that, thanks to the nymphs, " modern love " was no longer

> " *A fire celestial, chaste, refined,*
> *Conceived and kindled in the mind,*"

but had become a " gross desire," moving through caprice and folly. Venus, unable to decide the suit, had undertaken an experiment, and had endowed Vanessa, happily new-born, with all the virtues which the Queen of Love—or Swift—thought most " lovely in the female kind " : " a sweetness above all perfumes," a cleanliness " incapable of outward stains," a mind as modest as " the speech of prudes," and a " gentle, soft, engaging air." Not yet satisfied, Venus had fooled Pallas into thinking that the baby was a boy, and had obtained for her the other virtues " for manly bosoms chiefly fit " : " knowledge, judgment, wit," " justice, truth, and fortitude," " honour which no breath can

stain," " open heart and bounteous hand," and, since
" meat must be with money bought," as Pallas knew,
" some small regard for state and wealth " and a
useful fortune of five thousand pounds.

The romantic Venus, when all this was done, had
looked for the restoration of her power. The realistic
Pallas—

> " *For how can heavenly wisdom prove*
> *An instrument to earthly love ? "*—

had, though enraged by the deceit, left " all things to
their natural course." And Pallas was justified. The
beaux, when Vanessa came to town, listened to her
hermaphroditic discourses—

> " *Through nature and through art she ranged,*
> *And gracefully her subject changed "*—

and thought her tiresome. The belles, disgusted by her
lack of interest in clothes and gossip, thought her old-
fashioned.

> " *To copy her few nymphs aspired ;*
> *Her virtues fewer swains admired.*"

Vanessa hardened her heart and turned her back on
the world.

Was the actual Vanessa, when she had read this far,
pleased with the figure she cut in the fable ? Or did
the actual Cadenus, if he read it to her, notice that she
twisted in her chair ?

The verses went on. Cupid, zealous for his mother's
credit, resolved to conquer the adamant Vanessa. At

first he wasted shaft after shaft. Cadenus, the girl's tutor, protected her by "placing still some book betwixt" her and the mischievous god. Cupid saw he must include the tutor in his revenge. At a time when Cadenus—

> " *Grown old in politics and wit,*
> *Caressed by ministers of state,*
> *Of half mankind the dread and hate* "—

was reading to her, on her demand, from his "poetic works," Cupid shot a dart of such length that it pierced the volume and, carrying with it "some lines more moving than the rest," reached Vanessa's heart. Unlucky Vanessa.

> " *Cadenus, common forms apart,*
> *In every scene had kept his heart,*
> *Had sighed and languished, vowed and writ,*
> *For pastime, or to shew his wit,*
> *But books and time and state affairs*
> *Had spoiled his fashionable airs.*
> *He now could praise, esteem, approve,*
> *But understood not what was love.*
> *His conduct might have made him styled*
> *A father, and the nymph his child.*
> *That innocent delight he took*
> *To see the virgin mind her book*
> *Was but the master's secret joy*
> *In school to hear the finest boy.* "

Not having seen the malevolent arrow, he was amazed at the sudden change in his pupil. She seemed to listen more than ever but she could not keep her mind on what he said. Modestly he conjectured that he had bored her with studies too grave for her "tender sex and age." He should have known better. "Nature must be nature still." If she would excuse him, he would take his leave. But Vanessa, it soon appeared, had learned what he had taught her.

> " *Now, said the nymph, to let you see*
> *My actions with your rules agree,*
> *That I can vulgar forms despise,*
> *And have no secrets to disguise . . .*
> *Your lessons found the weakest part,*
> *Aimed at the head but reached the heart.*"

Cadenus was overwhelmed with " shame, disappointment, guilt, surprise." He could not doubt her words, but he thought he must pretend to, out of policy. The difference in their ages was too great. Love between them would be a scandal. He told her she must not seem so tragic when, as he knew, she was only joking.

Vanessa was too good a disputant to be put off. Reason, she insisted, was her guide in love. In loving him she was only loving the virtues and merits which she had observed in him and had made her own. Her love was as strong as self-love, for it was that. She had seen him full of "love, esteem, and awe" for dead geniuses. Surely he would have felt the same emotions if he had lived when they did. Then consider her case. She lived in the same age with a great genius. It was as much her duty as her instinct to adore him.

" *Cadenus answers every end,*
  The book, the author, and the friend.
  The utmost her desires will reach
  Is but to learn what he can teach.
  His converse is a system fit
  Alone to fill up all her wit,
  While every passion of her mind
  In him is centred and confined."

In that flood of reasons Cadenus wavered. They
were his own reasons, thrown back at him with his
skill. He could not think them bad reasons. He was
proud of his pupil for her eloquence. His pride, called
up by her, stayed to caress him. If he had been preferred to all the " colonels, lords, and beaux " by " so
bright a nymph " whom he had never thought of
courting, he must have the qualities which she saw in
him.

" '*Tis an old maxim in the schools*
  That flattery's the food of fools,
  Yet now and then your men of wit
  Will condescend to take a bit."

Cadenus could not withstand her tribute. Love, of
course, was out of the question.

" *Love why do we one passion call*
  When 'tis a compound of them all ?
  Where hot and cold, where sharp and sweet,
  In all their equipages meet,
  Where pleasure mixed with pains appear,
  Sorrow with joy, and hope with fear,
  Wherein his dignity and age
  Forbid Cadenus to engage."

But he could offer friendship, "a constant, rational delight," which was rooted in virtue and so could last, as shifting love could not. ' "Gratitude, respect, esteem " : those she could have to make up for his want of passion. He talked high about friendship.

Vanessa brought him down. If he was to give her "devotion, duty, and respect," their rôles would be changed. She would, however, take him at his word. He could be pupil and she be tutor, though she could see already that he would have a hard time with the science she had in mind for him. Any fool knew more than Cadenus about love.

The actual Vanessa, reading or listening, must have nodded, not with sleep. Did she stamp when the poem broke off?

> " *But what success Vanessa met*
> *Is to the world a secret yet.*
> *Whether the nymph to please her swain*
> *Talks in a high romantic strain,*
> *Or whether he at last descends*
> *To act with less seraphic ends,*
> *Or, to compound the business, whether*
> *They temper love and books together,*
> *Must never to mankind be told,*
> *Nor shall the conscious Muse unfold.*"

Did the reader or the listener follow the last lines of the fable, in which, with another flourish of contemporary grace, Venus decided against the shepherds, said her experiment had failed, left the world in the hands of her son, " harnessed her doves, and flew to heaven " ?

The tragedy of Vanessa was that Swift saw their drama as a comedy. Experience had fortified him against this scene. With Stella—

> *" When men began to call me fair*
> *You interposed your timely care "*—

Swift had already played Cadenus. If his temper had ever inclined him to love, or if his years had left him more audacity, or if he had been less absorbed in the great campaign of his pride, he might have responded to Vanessa—or if, of course, he had felt for her that kind of passion which makes the sun, or the moon, of a fresh love seem to shine on an earth just created. He met none of these conditions. He had an impulse to regulate her mind, but not to possess her person. He even believed that the desire he had was more important than the one he lacked. Cold towards Vanessa as flesh and blood, he was warm only towards the idea of being loved by her.

It was his pride which glowed. If, at the declaration, he had either loved or hated Vanessa he would have known what to do. He would have taken her or he would have gone from her, in the storm of any consequences. As it was, he let his pride seduce him as she could not. Its device was simple. It argued with him, as no doubt Vanessa did, that her fiery need of him obliged him to be kind. He hesitated. She was quick to snatch at her advantage. Give her the present, and she would not worry about the future. Give her what he could give, and she would not ask for more. These were promises which no shrewd man would have

151

trusted. He would have seen through them to what lay behind : the hope that if he could be held he could be won : the assurance that any kindness he might show would be more than kindness, would be the selfishness which she longed to find in him. Swift was not shrewd. Moved if not convinced, he agreed to do what he could to please her, not realizing how much it was to indulge himself.

Then, almost as if to clear himself of a last annoying suspicion, he told the story of Cadenus and Vanessa in the bold but humorous light in which he saw it. Such lucidity as his would have overpowered a stronger woman than Vanessa. Whether his version was at all points accurate or not, she had to fall into the place which his comedy had assigned her.

But she could struggle. The rest of her life was largely taken up by her efforts to get out of the poem and nearer to the poet. Swift, having made the blunder of undertaking to meet love with kindness, could never undo it. Vanessa pursued him like the ghost of his blunder. In August 1714, when he had sullenly retired to Berkshire, she surprised him with a visit. " You should not have come by Wantage for a thousand pound. You used to brag you were very discreet. Where is it gone ? " As soon as he had settled in Ireland, Vanessa followed. Her mother, having died, had left the daughters something of a fortune, including a handsome house at Celbridge eleven miles out of Dublin. From her house in the country or from occasional lodgings in town Vanessa implored him.

" Once I had a friend that would see me sometimes,

and either commend what I did or advise me what to do, which banished all my uneasiness. But now, when my misfortunes are increased by being in a disagreeable place, amongst strange, prying, deceitful people, whose company is so far from an amusement that it is a very great punishment, you fly me, and give me no reason but that we are amongst fools and must submit. I am very well satisfied that we are amongst such, but know no reason for having my happiness sacrificed to their caprice. You once had a maxim, which was to act what was right and not mind what the world said. I wish you would keep to it now. Pray what can be wrong in seeing and advising an unhappy young woman ? I can't imagine. You can't but know that your frowns make my life insupportable. You have taught me to distinguish and then you leave me miserable."

Swift answered only that he had " ever feared the tattle of this nasty town, and told you so." He begged her to be easy if he saw her still less often. " These are accidents in life that are necessary and must be submitted to."

Vanessa was not so frantic that she could mistake disinclination for discretion. " You bid me be easy, and you'd see me as often as you could. You had better said as often as you could get the better of your inclinations so much, or as often as you remembered that there was such a one in the world. If you continue to treat me as you do you will not be made uneasy by me long. 'Tis impossible to describe what I have suffered since I saw you last. I am sure I could have bore the

rack better than those killing, killing words of yours.
Sometimes I have resolved to die without seeing you
more ; but those resolves, to your misfortune, did not
last long. . . . The reason I write to you is because I
cannot tell it you, should I see you. For when I begin
to complain, then you are angry, and there is something in your look so awful that it strikes me dumb.
. . . I say as little as ever I can. Did you but know
what I thought I am sure it would move you. Forgive
me, and believe I cannot help telling you this and
live."

There are ways to get rid of importunate Vanessas,
but they are ways unknown to men who can try to be
kind to women desperately in love with them. Swift,
with his variations of temper, was the worst man in the
world for this Vanessa. In one letter he could write :
" A fig for your letters and messages " ; and in another :
" I cannot see you, I fear, to-day, having affairs of my
place to do ; but pray think it not want of friendship
or tenderness, which I will always continue to the
utmost." Vanessa, prying into every sentence to see
what might be hidden in it, turning every word over
and over with a lover's feverish research, could arrive
at the security neither of hope nor of despair.

The affair dragged on, irresistible passion matched
with immovable affection. Swift was Dean of St.
Patrick's, known to be the friend, and by some gossips
thought to be the husband, of Stella, who, though she
did not live at the deanery, was the centre of such life
as it had. He refused to give the world the least excuse
for regarding Vanessa as his mistress. He smothered

her with discretion, hating it yet unable to take a final
stand at one extremity or another. When he had
snubbed her long enough to put an end to any ordinary
suit, he would turn kind, would insist upon his esteem
and admiration, and so would once more rouse her.
He could or would not learn that her love and his
kindness were oil and water.

During the half-dozen dark years after he left the
Court for Ireland he perversely relished the secret
drama, whatever form it took, and let himself be
drawn into various cautious meetings with Vanessa.
When, towards the end of that eclipse, he began to be
more thoroughly himself, he became less cautious. His
whole nature, as if by some rejuvenation, expanded.
He took up the cause of Ireland against the Whigs. He
wrote verses, tender, intimate, teasing, to Stella. As
if he thought the conflict between him and Vanessa
was settled, he tried to get back to the old footing.

Instantly her desire flared up. " I here tell you,"
she wrote to him, " that I have determined to try all
manner of human arts to reclaim you." He did what
he could to laugh off her seriousness, even to praising
the art with which she wrote. Nothing would now
quiet her. His least kindness intoxicated her. When
he told her to use assumed names in her letters, which
he was afraid might be opened, and dashes for " everything that may be said to Cad—— at beginning or
conclusion," she was suddenly in raptures over sharing
secrets with him. "————Cad——, you are good
beyond expression, and I will never quarrel again if I
can help it." Swift did not take warning.

" What would you give," he asked her in August
1720, " to have the history of Cad—— and ——
exactly written, through all its steps, from the beginning to this time ? I believe it would do well in verse,
and be as long as the other. I hope it will be done. It
ought to be an exact chronicle of twelve years, from the
time of spilling the coffee to drinking of coffee, from
Dunstable to Dublin, with every single passage since.
There would be the chapter of the blister ; the chapter
ot Madam going to Kensington ; the chapter of the
Colonel's going to France ; the chapter of the wedding,
with the adventure of the lost key ; of the strain ; of
the joyful return ; two hundred chapters of madness ;
the chapter of long walks ; the Berkshire surprise ;
fifty chapters of little times ; the chapter of Chelsea ;
the chapter of swallow and cluster ; a hundred whole
books of myself and so low ; the chapter of hide and
whisper ; the chapter of Who made it so ? My sister's
money."

Vanessa, answering that " it would be too much
once to hope for such a history," asked him " did those
circumstances crowd on you, or did you recollect them
to make me happy ? " But, though she might suspect
that he had meant to please her, she could not help
exulting that he had remembered. She was not sure
friendship had such a memory. She knew love
had.

Swift had suggested that he might, for the first time,
visit her at Celbridge. " Is it possible you will come
and see me ? I beg for God sake you will." He did
visit her. Back in Dublin he advised her to take more

exercise, be cheerful, " read pleasant things that will make you laugh, and not sit moping with your elbows on your knees on a little stool by the fire."

Vanessa was out of hand. " I . . . here declare that 'tis not in the power of art, time, or accident to lessen the unexpressible passion which I have for — — —. Put my passion under the utmost restraint, send me as distant from you as the earth will allow, yet you cannot banish those charming ideas which will ever stick by me whilst I have the use of memory. Nor is the love I bear you only seated in my soul, for there is not a single atom of my frame that is not blended with it. . . . For heaven's sake tell me what has caused this prodigious change in you which I have found of late. If you have the least remains of pity for me left, tell me tenderly. No, don't tell it so that it may cause my present death ; and don't suffer me to lead a life like a languishing death, which is the only life I can lead if you have lost any of your tenderness for me."

Swift did not reply. The death of Vanessa's sister revived the correspondence, which went on with the same disparity. " The worst thing in you and me," he wrote, " is that we are too hard to please, and whether we have not made ourselves is the question. . . . We differ prodigiously in one point : I fly from the spleen to the world's end, you run out of your way to meet it." He urged her—Swift of all men—to accept what came and be pleased with it. She did her best to be the kind of philosopher he specified, but " I find the more I think the more unhappy I am."

In his last surviving letter to her he reminded her of the pleasant episodes " of Windsor, Cleveland Row, Ryder Street, St. James's, Kensington, the Sluttery, the Colonel in France. . . . Cad thinks often of these, especially on horseback, as I am assured. What a foolish thing is time, and how foolish is man who would be as angry if time stopped as if it passed." This was in August 1722. Vanessa died in June 1723.

The end of the story is all gossip. It says that Vanessa, unable to endure her jealousy, wrote to Swift, or to Stella, asking if it were true that Stella was Swift's wife. It says in one account that Stella answered that she was, in another that she sent the letter to Swift to answer. It says that Swift took the letter from Vanessa to Stella, or to him, and with it rode savagely to Celbridge, entered the room where Vanessa was, threw down the letter, gave Vanessa a look which for the last time struck her dumb and, without one of his " killing, killing words," left the house. It says that Vanessa thereupon changed her will, leaving her fortune to strangers, not to Swift, and died.

All gossip, any of it true, or none. Vanessa did leave her fortune to strangers and did not mention Swift among the friends to whom she gave small legacies to buy mourning rings. Something had parted Cadenus and Vanessa before she died. The parting was natural, but tragically late. She had loved a man whose thoughts, she said, " no human creature is capable of guessing at, because never any one living thought like you." She had spent her life trying to win him, and he had let her spend it. Dying, she planned what revenge was left to her, the publication of his poem about Cadenus and Vanessa and of the letters between them.

When the poem, though not the letters, appeared in 1726 to the comfort of his enemies, Swift kept silence. It had been, he told a friend, a " cavalier business," " a private humoursome thing which by an accident inevitable and the baseness of particular malice " had been made public. " I never saw it since I writ it." He refused to " use shifts or arts " to justify himself. " Let people think of me as they please. . . . I have borne a great deal more." He had gone through what was comedy for him and tragedy for Vanessa. Others must make up their own minds, if they had them, about who was to blame, if there must be blame, when a universal Héloïse encountered a special Abélard.

3

With whatever remorse, with whatever relief, with whatever concern for scandal, Swift the day after Vanessa's death left Dublin for the south of Ireland. Stella and Dingley were to spend the summer in the country at a friend's house. About Vanessa, so far as any record shows, Swift was silent, except to refer in a letter to her " incontinence in keeping secrets." And Stella was silent, except to remark, when she heard her rival praised, that the Dean could write finely about a broomstick. If there was between Swift and Stella such silence about Vanessa as they kept towards the world it was a silence beyond conjecture. The facts are drama enough. Stella went noiselessly in one direction. Swift went restlessly in another.

By the end of June he had made his way past Cork and had written a Latin poem on the rocks at Carbery where the ocean tore at the cliffs. By the beginning of August he had come up the west to Galway, still a hundred miles from home and "half weary of the four hundred I have rid." Late in September he was back in Dublin. Stella returned to town. Swift greeted her with his old raillery. She had been spoiled, he said, by the " generous wines and costly cheer " of Wood Park, and tried to ape them on her income.

> "*Thus for a week the farce went on;*
> *When, all her country savings gone,*
> *She fell into her former scene,*
> *Small beer, a herring, and the Dean:*"

It happened that during his absence from Dublin both Pope and Bolingbroke, and a little later Arbuthnot, took up the correspondence which they, and Swift more than they, had recently neglected. Fresh memories of England stirred in him. He exchanged affectionate letters with the Duchess of Ormond and Lady Masham. He wrote to Oxford demanding the bribe of a letter and a picture, "for who else knows how to deliver you down to posterity?" Bolingbroke had written : " I have vowed to read no history of our own country till that body of it which you promise to finish appears." Swift thought often of making himself the real historiographer of those buried, unforgotten years, in spite of the dullard who had the title. But he

160

was not yet ready for history. He was still alive to the events passing under his bitter eyes.

Swift hated Ireland because it was his place of banishment : " the whole kingdom a bare face of nature, without houses or plantations ; filthy cabins, miserable, tattered, half-starved creatures, scarce in human shape ; one insolent, ignorant, oppressive squire to be found in twenty miles riding ; a parish church to be found only in a summer day's journey, in comparison with which an English farmer's barn is a cathedral ; a bog of fifteen miles round ; every meadow a slough, and every hill a mixture of rock, heath, and marsh ; and every male and female, from the farmer inclusive to the day-labourer, infallibly a thief and consequently a beggar, which in this island are terms convertible." " The old seats of the nobility and gentry all in ruins, and no new ones in their stead." " The wretched merchants, instead of being dealers, are dwindled to pedlars and cheats." As to trade, " nothing worth mentioning except the linen of the north, a trade casual, corrupted, and at mercy, and some butter from Cork." The ports and harbours were of no more use " than a beautiful prospect to a man shut up in a dungeon." Travellers never came to Ireland, since they might expect to find there nothing but misery and desolation. Whoever could leave the kingdom left at the first chance and stayed away till the last excuse. Dublin was a " beggarly city," one-seventh of its houses falling in ruins, its populace hungry, idle, dissolute, dirty, and noisy. Though it was the capital of an ancient kingdom, the government was wholly in the hands of Englishmen who, blind to every interest but their own, lived there as little as they could manage.

No theoretical doctrine of liberty moved Swift to take up the Irish cause. " I do profess without affectation," he explained to Pope, " that your kind opinion of me as a patriot, since you call it so, is what I do not deserve ; because what I do is owing to perfect rage and resentment, and the mortifying sight of slavery, folly, and baseness about me, among which I am forced to live."

On the Catholic majority, those " savage old Irish," he spent little sympathy. They might be above the vermin of the island but they were below the voters. He had no patience with the Dissenters. They were outside the Church and to that extent outside his Ireland. Ireland for him was the English settled there, the noblemen, the landlords, the clergy, the lawyers, the merchants. Their ancestors had come to rule the conquered province. They themselves ought now to rule it. Instead, they were called Irish, which they were not, and in turn were ruled by the newest English, a changing garrison of place-men. Men born in Ireland could not hope for posts at home. They had either to rot on their estates or to go abroad while their tenants were racked to support them in a dingy splendour. The Irish Parliament had no power. The laws, all made in England, condemned Ireland to poverty. Cattle could not be shipped to England, woollen goods could not be shipped anywhere. Without a free hand in agriculture, manufacture, or trade,

Ireland from being so long bound was numb or sodden.

Mortified by finding himself in exile among slaves, Swift first despised them and then hated their tyrants. The tyrants were the Whigs who had driven him out of power. He could not become a slave. He could not endure a tyrant. Everything in his nature urged him to rouse the slaves and resist the tyrants. But he had the advantage, when he turned his fury loose, of a long experience in hating the party to which his enemies belonged.

Where his whole cause was so good Swift did not need to be fastidious about his particular occasion for attack. William Wood, an English ironmonger, in 1722 obtained a patent from the King to coin half-pence and farthings for Ireland for fourteen years. The Irish were not agreed that they needed new copper coins, certainly not to the amount of a hundred thousand pounds. The Irish were not consulted, nor even the Lord-Lieutenant. Higher interests were involved. The patent had really been granted to the Duchess of Kendal, the King's mistress, who sold it to Wood for ten thousand pounds. Walpole, Lord Treasurer, did not object. The Duchess had been loyal. The King was grateful. Through the method of the patent she could be rewarded, not by the King directly but indirectly by his Irish subjects, who already, if they had known it, contributed three thousand annually in pensions to the loyal lady. Since there was some risk, Wood deserved a profit for his trouble. The necessary copper would cost him sixty thousand pounds. When he had satisfied the Duchess he would still have thirty thousand, of which perhaps one-fifth would pay for the coinage and about one-seventh go to fees required by the patent. As jobs went in the government of Ireland under Walpole, the profit was not unheard of.

But the failure to consult the Irish had angered them. Their Parliament protested to the Treasury. Lord Carteret, a friend of Swift and now Secretary of State, was at odds with Walpole. Walpole, persisting, got Carteret appointed Lord-Lieutenant early in 1724, to get rid of him in London. By the time he reached Dublin the whole country was in a passion.

The passion was led and guided by Swift. Walpole's scheme, shabby, cynical, insulting, brought the satirist with a roar out of his long silence. He was as crafty as he was furious. Pretending to be a small tradesman named Drapier, he addressed, between April and November 1724, a series of letters to the shopkeepers, tradesmen, farmers, and common people, to his printer, to the nobility and gentry, to the whole people of Ireland. He was as furious as he was crafty. Wood was a " single, diminutive, insignificant mechanic." He and his agents, trying to force upon the Irish the coins which the patent did not oblige them to accept, were " enemies to God and this kingdom." " I will shoot Mr. Wood and his deputies through the head, like highwaymen or housebreakers, if they dare to force one farthing of their coin upon me in the payment of an hundred pounds. It is no loss of honour to submit to the lion, but who, with the figure of a man, can think with patience of being devoured alive by a rat." " I entreat you, my dear countrymen, not to be under the least concern upon these and the like rumours, which are no more than the last howls of a dog dissected alive, as I hope he hath sufficiently been."

Swift did not dare to accuse the King, and he only hinted at the honorarium to the Duchess. It was the ministers who had planned this contemptuous oppression. It was Wood who was to his own advantage carrying it out at the expense of Ireland. If Wood's copper became current every Irishman who received a coin, even in the smallest transaction, would get less than he gave, and every Irishman who paid out a coin would give less than he got. While Wood prospered " we should live together as merry and sociable as beggars, only with this one abatement, that we should have neither meat to feed nor manufactures to clothe us, unless we could be content to prance about in coats of mail or eat brass as ostriches do iron."

Swift must have known that his arguments were false, must have known that the intrinsic value of such small coins did not matter and that they would be as good as any if they were used. He who gave and he who got could not be equally losers. But Swift did not boggle over economic niceties. Here was a principle. To accept the coins would be to surrender to tyrants and become slaves. As soon as he had stirred the public to a fear of losing money and had assured them they could lawfully refuse the new halfpence and farthings, he moved towards a general position.

" Were not the people of Ireland born as free as

those of England ? How have they forfeited their freedom ? Is not their Parliament as fair a representative
of the people as that of England ? . . . Are they not
subjects of the same king ? Does not the same sun
shine upon them ? And have they not the same God
for their protector ? Am I a freeman in England, and
do I become a slave in six hours by crossing the
channel ? " " I have looked over all the English and
Irish statutes without finding any law that makes
Ireland depend upon England any more than England
does upon Ireland. We have indeed obliged ourselves
to have the same king with them, and consequently
they are obliged to have the same king with us. For the
law was made by our own ancestors, and our ancestors
then were not such fools (whatever they were in the
preceding reign) to bring themselves under I know not
what dependence which is now talked of without any
ground of law, reason, or common sense." " All
government without the consent of the governed is the
very definition of slavery." " The remedy is wholly in
your own hands. . . . By the laws of God, of Nature,
of nations, and of your own country you are and ought
to be as free a people as your brethren in England."

No voice like this had ever been raised by an Eng-
lishman in Ireland. All the Irish heard it. Never
again were its echoes to be long silent in that country.
" Money," Swift said, " the great divider of the world,
hath by a strange revolution been the great uniter of a
most divided people."

On the day Carteret landed in October the fourth
and most thoroughgoing of the Drapier letters was

issued. Hawkers crying it through the streets met the Lord-Lieutenant when he arrived in Dublin. Much as Carteret admired " that genius which has outshone most of this age and when you will display it again can convince us that its lustre and strength are still the same," he could not, in his station, overlook the Drapier. He offered a reward of three hundred pounds for information leading to the discovery of the author within six months. All Dublin, including the Lord-Lieutenant, knew that Swift had written the dangerous letters. But there was no legal proof, even if there was anywhere an informer. During the six months Swift dined at the Castle and entertained Lady Carteret at a party in his garden. When Carteret heard that Swift had " some thoughts of declaring himself " he advised against it. Their friendship, however, was not tested to the utmost. Walpole, seeing that the case was hopeless in such a tumult, gave it up. The patent was withdrawn in 1725 as an instance of royal favour and condescension. Wood was compensated with a pension of three thousand pounds a year for twelve years. Carteret later summed up his administration : " The people ask me how I governed Ireland. I say that I pleased Dr. Swift."

Swift, writing to Oxford's son, apologized for his mention of the Irish brawl. " This is just of as much consequence to your Lordship as the news of a skirmish between two petty states in Greece was to Alexander while he was conquering Persia, but even a knot of beggars are of importance among themselves." Yet Swift was too much a soldier not to enjoy a battle after a stupid peace. Though there were others in the field, he unmistakably commanded. The Grand Jury and the Liberty of St. Patrick's, that part of Dublin over which he as Dean had civil jurisdiction, formally resolved against the hated coins, as did the butchers, the brewers, the newsboys or " flying stationers," and the Black Guard. There were broadsheets on every corner, songs in every tavern, some of them written by Swift, all of them in support of the Drapier. While the furore lasted no jury would find anything seditious in any pamphlet or lampoon if Wood were mentioned. After the victory medals were struck in the Drapier's honour, shops and taverns were named for him, women carried handkerchiefs with his picture woven on them. Something legendary began to enlarge Swift's fame.

Irishmen who could barely spell out his arguments and knew only by hearsay that he was a man of learning who had been great in London were roused to veneration. They had thought of him as one of their rulers sent from England, yet he had joined their cause against the English. He was not a tyrant but a patriot. Standing superbly against the dread, incalculable ministers, he had defended men and women to whom halfpence and farthings were important. They stood uncovered when he passed in the streets.

They could not know that he had acted, at least at first, out of hate for their slavery and folly and baseness, out of a fierce unwillingness to be slavish and foolish and base along with them. He who had had a hand in ruling an empire would not submit to being counted among the docile subjects of the province to which he had been banished. Private resentment had stirred him to public rebellion. He could not help it if what he had done for hate was the same as if he had done it for love. Such an outcome was only another proof that the world was wrong. Like Gulliver in Lilliput, wading home with the Blefuscudian fleet at the end of a packthread, Swift decently exulted. But he would not let himself forget that the adventure had taken place among the pigmies. Whatever he accomplished was a small affair. Great affairs were always maddeningly beyond him, or, he remembered his days with Oxford, behind him.

VI

TRAVELLER

I

s w i f t never set a foot outside Ireland or England
except when he hurried across Wales on his restless
journeys between London, the bright centre of his
world, and Dublin, the dreary margin. Though he
constantly diverted himself with books of travel, he
found in them nothing which convinced him that he
would anywhere meet more wisdom or less folly than
he everywhere observed. The Scotch were a " poor,
fierce northern people," the Dutch grasping and
shifty, the French frivolous and Catholic. If he had
some liking for the Swedes it was because he was
fascinated by Charles XII, that sudden, terrific king
who had burst upon Europe from his cold peninsula
and stirred philosophers to admiration by such a
career as Swift would have chosen for himself. But
dividing mankind into nations was little more than
drawing lines on a map. The whole earth was in-
habited by the human race.

Once Swift had hopes of going to Austria, once to
Sweden, once to France. Each time prevented, he
hardly grumbled. If he thought of other countries it
was for their better climate, which might, he said,

have kept his wit and humour lively, as Ireland's had
not. " I imagine," he wrote in 1724, " France would
be proper for me now, and Italy ten years hence."
But he could not rouse himself from thinking about the
world to travel far to look at it. There was his giddiness, which might at any time make him reel and fall.
There was his deafness, which forced him to live
" among those whom I can govern and make them
comply with my infirmities." There was the prospect
of blindness. " My eyes will not suffer me to read
small prints, nor anything by candlelight, and if I
grow blind, as well as deaf I must needs become very
grave and wise and insignificant." He was caged in
Ireland, with nothing to do but pace his cage.

In Ireland, however, Swift was not confined to the
cramped cottage at Laracor or to the hollow deanery
in Dublin. During the twelve unbroken years of his
banishment after 1714 he often visited other houses.
His hosts could never have enough of him. Near
Laracor were the houses of Peter Ludlow, George
Rochfort, and Knightley Chetwoode. Near Dublin
were the houses of the Grattans and Patrick Delaney
and Charles Ford, with whom Stella spent a summer.
Forty miles from Dublin was Thomas Sheridan's ram-
shackle house which Swift could sometimes have to
himself. He is said to have visited an ancestor of the
Earls of Llandaff in Tipperary. He visited the Ashes
—St. George Ashe had been Swift's college tutor—
at Clogher in Tyrone, Robert Cope in Armagh, the
Bishop of Dromore in Down. And during the summers
of 1722 and 1723, when banishment had become

lmost unendurable, Swift made long, lonely journeys o the north and to the south. " I have shifted scenes," he told Vanessa in July 1722, " oftener than I ever did in my life, and I believe I have lain in thirty beds since I left the town."

Six hundred miles in the north, five hundred in the south the year following, all solitary and speculative. But these were not merely random travels in search of change and health. Though Swift was still incorrigibly Swift, he was also Gulliver, now with a purpose studying the despicable ways of men.

Gulliver's travels were Swift's travels, disguised with Swift's wit, loaded with Swift's hate. He gave years to them, as to nothing else he ever wrote about, five or six years thinking of them as Martin Scriblerus's travels, nearly as long thinking of them as Gulliver's or his own. " I am now writing a History of my Travels," Swift told Ford in April 1721, " which will be a large volume, and gives account of countries hitherto unknown ; but they go on slowly for want of health and humour." By December of that year Bolingbroke knew about them. " I long to see your Travels ; for, take is as you will, I do not retract what I said, and will undertake to find in two pages of your bagatelles more good sense, useful knowledge, and true religion than you can show me in the works of nineteen in twenty of the profound divines and philosophers of the age." In June 1722 Vanessa had read something about the giants. In January 1724 Swift was near the end. " I have left the Country of Horses," he wrote to Ford, " and am in the Flying Island, where

I shall not stay long, and my two last journeys will soon be over." In July 1725 Bolingbroke referred to the pigmies and giants of which he had heard. In August, Swift wrote to Ford : " I have finished my Travels, and am now transcribing them. They are admirable things, and will wonderfully mend the world."

In September, after a summer at Sheridan's house in the country, Swift wrote to Pope : " I have employed my time, besides ditching, in finishing, correcting, amending, and transcribing my Travels, in four parts complete, newly augmented, and intended for the press when the world shall deserve them, or rather when a printer shall be found brave enough to venture his ears." Thereafter all Swift's friends waited to see how he would, as he said, " vex the world rather than divert it." They could be sure he had written more than a story of imaginary voyages in a book. This would be Swift's revenge.

In the days of the Scriblerus Club it had been planned that Martin on his first voyage should be carried " by a prosperous storm to a discovery of the ancient Pygmean empire " ; on his second should be " happily shipwrecked on the land of the giants, the most humane people in the world " ; on his third should reach a " kingdom of philosophers who govern by the mathematics " ; and on his fourth should, among beings not yet named, " display a vein of melancholy proceeding almost to a disgust of his species." These plans had broken up with the Club. Returning to this theme, Swift saw that the bungling Martin would no longer serve. If he were to be the traveller, much of the folly of the narrative would have to appear in his misadventures. Better to let the traveller be a plain, reasonable, unimaginative man who would report what he had seen in the language of common sense.

Swift's nature included such a Gulliver. It included, too, an observer as alien to what went on around him as Gulliver could be on his most distant, most surprising island. " My disaffection to the world . . . has never varied from the twenty-first . . . year of my life." Disaffection, singularity, had driven Swift, no less than most men, to think of himself as playing various rôles. At Kilkenny and Trinity he had been a tragic hero, neglected and abused by fortune. At Moor Park he had been a scholar in a garden, despising the rabble of wits and pedants. At Laracor he had been a soldier in a garrison, when there were wars elsewhere. In London he had been the conscience and voice of ministers, insisting upon order and virtue in the state. In Dublin, exiled, he had turned from governing to resisting and had made himself the hammer of tyrants. Now he was a creature of a different race, thrown among men, full of antipathy for them, but full also of a scornful curiosity.

It was the best rôle he ever found. Without once taking the ship to the corners of the earth as Gulliver did, Swift had moved about at home too large for the pigmies, too small for the giants, too sensible for the philosophers, too human for the animals. He had never been able quite to adjust himself to the scale of life as other men lived it. Other men, even when they had the pride of distinction, could submit. Swift could not. As if he were really an alien to the race, he had been obliged, whether he chose or not, to feel and act alien. Only once in more than fifty years had he found an occupation which truly involved him, and that only while a short delusion lasted. He had been unwilling to take a wife, though women desired and loved him. He had compromised so far as to have friends, but he was always conscious of the exceptions he was making. " I have ever hated all nations, professions, and communities, and all my love is towards individuals. . . . But principally I hate and detest that animal called man, although I heartily love John, Peter, Thomas, and so forth. This is the system upon which I have governed myself many years. . . . Upon this great foundation of misanthropy . . . the whole building of my Travels is erected ; and I will never have peace of mind till all honest men are of my opinion."

If he had been fully alien he would not have troubled himself to be a missionary. He was a man to the extent that he was a moralist as well as a misanthrope. He would cure if he could. If not, he would punish. " Drown the world ! I am not content with despising it, but I would anger it if I could with safety." Here was the flaw in his misanthropy. Here was the strain of humanity through which he could be fretted and hurt. Here was the deep source of his fury. But he was alien enough to feel, dramatically, that he was only a traveller in strange lands.

Yet Swift was not a Timon, bawling and railing.

Swift's misanthropy was in his constitution, not in his disposition. His friends spoke always of his sweetness, his charm, his delightful temper, his hearty affections, his honest generosity. He had about him a magic almost like beauty's magic. Nor did they think of him as morose and surly, whatever he said about himself. " Gulliver is a happy man," said the experienced Arbuthnot, " that at his age can write such a merry work." Swift on his travels could no more help the wit on his tongue than he could help the detestation in his heart.

He was as ingenious as he was grave. He took pains, with a few slips, to draw his pigmies and giants to scale, the pigmies an inch to a human foot, the giants a foot to a human inch. He deftly commandeered the inventions of earlier writers : Philostratus, Lucian, Rabelais, Cyrano de Bergerac, Perrot d'Ablancourt, Tom Brown. The nautical terms paraded in the voyage to Brobdingnag were copied almost word for word from a mariner's handbook. Swift did not disdain to parody contemporary travellers. Whereas a mere misanthrope would have clamoured, a mere moralist would have scolded, Swift, being a wit, was satisfied to tell a story, pretending that he was a spectator who had no share in what he told. There were the characters, there were the incidents. They could be understood by anybody who had an understanding.

Consider the insectile people of Lilliput. Swift, in the guise of Gulliver, was at first received with dread, then with wonder, then with hospitality. Though they

kept him a prisoner, they let him into the secrets of
the Court and of the government, which were pre-
posterously like England's. The Lilliputian ministers
to commend themselves to the king capered before him
on a tight-rope. Gulliver, whose mind was part of
Swift's, remembered larger ministers. Flimnap, who
could caper an inch higher than any other lord in the
empire, seemed remarkably like Walpole. The great
men of Lilliput who sought honours from their king
competed, by jumping over a stick held in his hand,
for silken threads six inches long, one blue, one red,
one green, which reminded Gulliver of the Order of
the Garter, of the Bath, and of the Thistle.

Lilliput and the neighbouring Blefuscu had long
been at war. A Lilliputian schism was the cause.
Formerly all the people had broken their eggs at the
larger end. One of their kings, having cut his finger
on the larger end of one of his eggs, had by royal edict
made the smaller end orthodox. There had been a
civil war. Some of the defeated conservatives had fled
to Blefuscu and had there found refuge and favour at
the court. England, Gulliver reflected, had been
entirely Catholic before Henry VIII. The Catholic
Pretender had fled to France, and France had long
been at war with England.

Grateful for the kindness shown him, Gulliver aided
Lilliput in its war by capturing the Blefuscudian fleet
and bringing it as a gift to his royal host. But the
Lilliputians were no more grateful in return than the
English had been to the Oxford Ministry for ending
the war with France. One party among the pigmies

insisted that Blefuscu be subjugated to a province with a viceroy, as some of the Whigs had insisted France might be. The sourest of the tiny ministers became Gulliver's enemy, as the dismal Nottingham had become Swift's.

Gulliver's chief offence was that, when a fire broke out in the queen's apartment at the palace, he extinguished it in a manner more natural to him than agreeable to the queen. Had not Queen Anne implacably resented the spattering ridicule which Swift had let fall upon what he thought was menacing the Church and State ? Thereafter the position of Gulliver in Lilliput was hopeless. The cabinet decided he must die. The friendly minister Reldresal, who may have stood for Carteret, thought it would be enough to blind Gulliver and allow him to starve to death.

From that compromise Gulliver escaped to Blefuscu, and back to England, knowing that the smallest people in the world had all the familiar follies and vices of mankind in general.

Next Swift, as Gulliver, was blown to the giants of Brobdingnag, that humane people. It was his turn to be insectile. He was exhibited as a toy freak by the kind, greedy farmer who had found him. Scientists wondered what species he could belong to. The king, being a philosopher, supposed that such creatures as Gulliver " have their titles and distinctions of honour ; they contrive little nests and burrows that they call houses and cities ; they make a figure in dress and equipage ; they love, they fight, they dispute, they cheat, they betray." And when Gulliver had defended

his species by an account of their government and
politics, their wars and luxuries, the king, being a
humane philosopher, concluded " your natives to be
the most pernicious race of little odious vermin that
nature ever suffered to crawl upon the surface of the
earth."

He himself abominated mystery, refinement, and
intrigue in governors. He limited government " to
common sense and reason, to justice and lenity, to the
speedy determination of civil and criminal causes."
He held that " whoever could make two ears of corn or
two blades of grass grow upon a spot of ground where
only one grew before would deserve better of mankind
. . . than the whole race of politicians put together."
Gulliver, or Swift, sardonically despaired of such a
monarch. His people were no better. Their learning
was only in morality, history, poetry, and useful
mathematics. They were unable to form conceptions
of what Gulliver meant by " entities, abstractions, and
transcendentals." They were dull with virtue and
peace.

Gulliver found in their habits less to remind him of
England than he had found in Lilliput. His story was
taken up with the ingenious shifts by which he got
along among them. But after the giants he could not
so easily return to the old scale of life as he could after
the pigmies. His own people seemed contemptible by
their smallness. He was twice as far from mankind as
he had been before.

Swift's, Gulliver's, third voyage seems to have been
to the Country of Horses, but when he told the story

he saved that for the venomous conclusion and in the third place put the account of the Flying Island and the continent which was topsy-turvy with philosophers.

Once more, as in Lilliput, he was often reminded of Europe. The name of Laputa was like the Spanish for harlot. The island, when its rulers wished, could hover over stubborn cities and shut out the sun, as England shut out the sun from Ireland. Whether aloft or on land the people were rapt in abstruse speculations or abandoned to fantastic projects. Among the islanders nobody spoke sense except, possibly, the tradesmen, women, and children. The others were so many pedants exaggerated from the breed that Swift had detested in his earliest satires. The Academy of Lagado was a Bedlam of Science, where men wore out their lives trying to extract sunbeams from cucumbers, to build houses downward from the roofs in the fashion of the bees and spiders, to plough fields only with the snouts of hogs, to make silk from spider webs, to cure colic with a pair of bellows, to soften marble for pin-cushions, to propagate naked sheep, to write books by a mechanical device, to discover painless methods of taxation.

Gulliver grew dizzy. He lacked the head, as Swift did, for this whirling universe. It did not steady him when, on the neighbouring island of Glubbdubdrib, he was allowed to call up the spirits of the famous dead and found how falsely they had been presented in history. It did not steady him when in Luggnagg he learned of the immortal struldbrugs, for whom im-mortality was only human life prolonged to an infinity of horrible old age. " I . . . thought," said Gulliver, for Swift, " that no tyrant could invent a death into which I would not run with pleasure from such a life." When he was out of the mad lands of Laputa, Balni-barbi, Glubbdubdrib, and Luggnagg, he was nearly upside down, giddy, and three times as far from mankind.

Now for the antipodes of misanthropy. Among the Houyhnhnms Gulliver was almost undisguisedly Swift. The day on which Gulliver set sail from Portsmouth was the precise day of September 1710 on which Swift had arrived in London to make his fortune with the new men in power. Gulliver's discovery of an island where the horses were as much wiser and nobler as they were stronger than the men was such a dis-covery as Swift may have made as he rode through desolate, beggarly Ireland.

It is easy to guess, though only to guess, that the device came to his mind on that dark expedition to the south in the summer of 1723 after Vanessa's death. Everywhere he saw the " savage old Irish," " miserable, tattered, half-starved creatures, scarce in human shape," living " in the utmost ignorance, barbarity, and poverty, giving themselves wholly up to idleness, nastiness, and thievery," " brought up to steal or beg for want of work," so that to them " death would be the best thing to be wished for both on account of themselves and the public." Swift had not yet reached the point where he could take up the cause of these miserable victims. He felt chiefly a sick repulsion. He would not admit that they and he were of the same kind. At least they must belong to a tribe which had degenerated till they were less than beasts.

Less than beasts? Compare them with his horse, healthy, patient, without follies or vices, incapable of pride. Horses, the animals Swift had most to do with and knew best, were more fit to rule than degraded men. Suppose some traveller should find a country where the horses did rule. Suppose Gulliver were to find it. The Scriblerus Club had not decided what race Martin was to visit on his fourth voyage, only that he was to " display a vein of melancholy proceeding almost to a disgust of his species." Nothing could disgust a traveller, even wholesome Gulliver, more than to study the horrid antics of a debased human tribe in the company of utopian horses who could see little difference between him and those apish copies. Gulliver had been disgusted among the giants when the maids of honour laid him against their terrible breasts. That had been only a shrinking of his senses. Now his soul itself must shrink with an absolute antipathy from which he could not recover. When he came back he would prefer the horses of England to the men.

With something like these gathering plans, though they must be guessed at, in something like this mood, which is certain enough, Swift rode through the south and west. In September he was in Dublin again. By the next January he had " left the Country of Horses."

On his icy, fiery travels among the Houyhnhnms Swift (why call him Gulliver?) did not bother to observe such stinging likenesses to particular English persons and episodes as he observed among the pigmies and the philosophers. The last of his adventures was the simplest, as it was the most deadly. All actual fantasy, all apparent fact.

He came upon his first Yahoos without realizing that they were inferior men and upon his first Houyhnhnms without realizing that they were superior horses. When he found himself taken for a Yahoo he hurried to tell his Houyhnhnm master about Europe. He told him of wars, their causes, means, and ends ; of litigation and the arts of lawyers ; of money, and of poverty and riches ; of luxury and dissipation ; of diseases and their remedies ; of ministers of state and noblemen. The reasonable Houyhnhnm said he had noticed the rudiments of all these human ways of life among the Yahoos.

They had their tribal and civil wars. They hoarded shining stones which they could not use, fought over them, and sometimes lost them to bystanders who snatched them away as expertly as any lawyer. They gorged themselves with food and sucked a root that made them drunk. They had the only diseases in the country, because of their gluttony and filth. They had in most herds a sort of ruling Yahoo, always deformed in body and mischievous in disposition, who continued in office till a worse could be found. They were lewd and promiscuous. They were invariably dirty and sometimes splenetic. They had, it appeared, all the human vices except unnatural appetites, these " politer pleasures " not having occurred to them. They were unteachable because they were perverse and restive, but they had the brains to be cunning, malicious, treacherous, revengeful, insolent, abject, and cruel. It was plain to the Houyhnhnm who talked with Swift that the visitor was a Yahoo after all. That " small pittance of reason " which by some accident had been given to the European Yahoos they used only to multiply their natural corruptions and to acquire new ones not supplied by nature.

To be fully reasonable was to be like the Houyhnhnms. They did not know what lying was. They affirmed or denied only when they were certain. Their two principal virtues were friendship and benevolence, felt towards the whole species without partiality except where there were special virtues to attract them. In marriage they were without jealousy, fondness, quarrelling, or discontent. The young of both sexes were brought up in moderation, industry, exercise, and cleanliness. Their only government was an annual council of the entire nation. They had no literature except poems composed, not written down, in praise of virtue. They were skilful workmen in the necessary arts, but wasted no time on superfluity or show. Reasonably born and bred, they lived reasonably without passions and died reasonably without sickness or fear.

" At first, indeed, I did not feel that natural awe which the Yahoos and all other animals bear towards them ; but it grew upon me by degrees, much sooner than I imagined, and was mingled with a respectful love and gratitude that they would condescend to distinguish me from the rest of my species. When I thought of my family, my friends, my countrymen, or human race in general, I considered them as they really were, Yahoos in shape and disposition." Swift would have remained with the Houyhnhnms for ever if they had not sent him away. The beasts could not tolerate a man. Nor could a man who had lived among the beasts ever again live among men without disgust.

The fourth voyage marked the peak of Swift's fury and of his art. Great as that art was, it could not quite conceal that fury. The narrative might seem, however fantastic, to be the very mathematics of misanthropy, never looser than a syllogism. But the cold tread of intellect was repeatedly broken by the rush of nerves. The most reasonable sentence might suddenly throb with words of a shuddering hate. " Imagine twenty thousand of them breaking into the midst of an European army, confounding the ranks, overturning the carriages, battering the warriors' faces into mummy by terrible yerks from their hinder hoofs." Intellect would have been satisfied with beating the European Yahoos down ; nerves, furious and yet frightened at their own desperation, must imagine battering the noisome faces into mummy. Nothing less than an agonized antipathy could have made Swift remark that the female Yahoo who embraced Gulliver was not red-haired, " which might have been some excuse for an appetite a little irregular," but " black as a sloe "—or as Stella. Hate possessed him as love possesses some other men.

If he had been a lover of his kind he might have been hot with praises for the lofty merits which he found in them, and might have seen the world smirk at his tribute. Instead, he was a hater. Was there not as good an excuse for hating as for loving ? Was it any less accurate to perceive ugliness, deformity, vice, stupidity, loathsomeness in the human race than to perceive beauty, grace, virtue, wit, charm ? Swift would have known that these were absurd questions, asked to no purpose. Mankind would always answer them for its own comfort, which demands that love must be, in moral arguments, preferred to hate. The crowded tribes of the earth lived too precariously to welcome the hate, however instinctive, which might come among them to separate man from man, tribe from tribe, man from tribe. Only in the warmth of love could they live together. If the Swifts of the world must hate they must live alone, even if what they hated, as with Swift, was hate itself, along with cruelty, avarice, oppression, filth, intemperance, presumption.

All this Swift had learned. But he had no choice. His nature insisted upon taking its revenge as a coiled spring insists upon recoiling as soon as it is free. He had travelled through the world. He would tell the whole truth about his travels.

2

A man who had been around the world and under it might after twelve years of banishment venture from Ireland to London. Swift's friends had never ceased urging him to visit them again. He would only now and then allow himself to think of it.

186

" What can be the design of your letter but malice,"
he wrote to Gay in January 1723, " to wake me out of
a scurvy sleep, which however is better than none ?
. . . I shall not be able to relish my wine, my parsons,
my horses, nor my garden for three months, until the
spirit you have raised shall be dispossessed. I have
sometimes wondered that I have not visited you, but
I have been stopped by too many reasons, besides
years and laziness, and yet these are very good ones.
Upon my return after half a year amongst you there
would be to me *desiderio nec pudor nec modus*. I was three
years reconciling myself to the scene and the business
to which fortune has condemned me, and stupidity
was what I had recourse to. Besides, what a figure
should I make in London, while my friends are in
poverty, exile, distress, or imprisonment, and my
enemies with rods of iron ? Yet I often threaten myself
with the journey, and am every summer practising to
ride and get health to bear it. The only inconvenience
is that I grow old in the experiment."

But in November 1724, Oxford having died,
Oxford's son invited Swift to come to England to
write the biography which he had proposed. " There
would be nobody more welcome to me than yourself.
You should live in your own way and do just what
was most agreeable to you. I have houses enough ;
you shall take your choice." By September 1725 Swift
had his Travels ready to be printed. With two such
reasons for going he had no excuse for staying. His
friends urged him with fresh tenderness and wit.

" I have often imagined to myself," Pope wrote in

October, " that if ever all of us met again, after so many varieties and changes, after so much of the old world and of the old man in each of us has been altered, after there has been such a new heaven and a new earth in our minds and bodies that scarce a single thought of the one, any more than a single atom of the other, remains just the same—I have fancied, I say, that we should meet like the righteous in the millennium, quite in peace, divested of all our former passions, smiling at all our own designs, and content to enjoy the kingdom of the just in tranquillity."

Arbuthnot, just recovering from a nearly fatal illness, had intended to add a postscript to Pope's letter. He was so moved by what Swift had said—" Oh ! if the world had but a dozen Arbuthnots in it I would burn my Travels "—that he wrote a letter of his own. " For God's sake do not tantalize your friends any more. I can prove by twenty unanswerable arguments that it is absolutely necessary you should come over to England ; that it would be committing the greatest absurdity that ever was not to do it the next approaching winter. I believe, indeed, it is just possible to save your soul without it, and that is all."

Some feverish disorder kept Swift " sitting like a toad in a corner of his great house " for a part of that winter, but he had set his mind on England for the spring. " If you do not know me when we meet," he told Pope, " you need only keep one of my letters and compare it with my face, for my face and letters are counterparts of my heart." About the middle of March he was in London, in the best of health and spirits, Pope said, and " the joy of all here who know him, as he was eleven years ago."

There were two weeks of joyful, leisurely reunion. Pope left his villa for Swift's lodgings. Arbuthnot " led him a course through the town " with such new men of fashion as Lord Chesterfield and William Pulteney (later the Earl of Bath). Harcourt and Peterborough made plans to introduce him to Walpole ; Pope, though Arbuthnot got ahead of him, to the household of the Prince of Wales through Mrs. Howard, the Princess's confidante. Swift visited Bolingbroke and Pope in the country, and by the first of April was ready, with Pope, " to ramble to Lord Oxford's and Lord Bathurst's and other places." Pope found his guest " the best-natured and most indulgent man I know."

Swift had come into a world as strange to him as the world he had found in 1710. Though the Whigs were in power, they were not the Whigs he had known. Somers, Halifax, Wharton, and Addison were dead. Congreve was alive, but gouty and almost blind. Steele was alive, but in Wales and paralysed. The Tories Swift had known were scattered. Oxford had died, Ormond had settled in Spain, Bolingbroke, though pardoned and again in England, was excluded from the House of Lords. The Society of Brothers no longer dined together, men of influence with men of wit. Prior was dead.

Only in what had once been the Scriblerus Club was London much the same as Swift had left it, except that Parnell too was dead. Bolingbroke, formerly a kind of honorary member, now gave his time to

philosophizing near Uxbridge about the uses of retirement and scheming how to get back in power.
Pope, having made a fortune out of Homer, had
retired to his house and grotto at Twickenham and
was brewing poison for the dunces. Gay, with a small
sinecure and lodgings in the palace at Whitehall, was
completing the fables which he wrote for Prince
William, son of the Prince of Wales. Arbuthnot, still
as always a man of learning, virtue, sense and wit,
called his house in London Martin's office, though the
Scriblerus Club had given up its regular meetings.

Swift, being Swift, could not withhold himself from
politics. The authorities in Ireland warned the authorities in England to watch out for him. Walpole, who
may have wanted to win Swift over and who may have
wanted merely to learn about Irish affairs, invited
Swift to dine with him at Chelsea and later to call on
him in London. First and last they were at deadlock,
however, though scandal buzzed about a treaty between them. Walpole's opinions concerning Ireland,
Swift said, " I could not reconcile to the notions I had
of liberty." " I was neither offered nor would have
received " any promotion " except upon conditions
which would never be granted." By the end of April
he was " weary of being among ministers whom I
cannot govern, who are all rank Tories in government
and worse than Whigs in Church, whereas I was the
first man who taught and practised the direct contrary
principle." If he had any hope it was in the opposition
being organized by Pulteney and Sir William Wyndham, with the help and advice of Bolingbroke, and

with the name of the Patriots. But Swift's old zest, perhaps his old delusion, had gone.

" This is the first time I was ever weary of England and longed to be in Ireland," he wrote to Sheridan. " But it is because go I must, for I do not love Ireland better nor England, as England, worse. In short, you all live in a wretched, dirty doghole and prison, but it is a place good enough to die in. I can tell you one thing, that I have had the fairest offer made me of a settlement here that one can imagine, which if I were ten years younger I would gladly accept, within ten miles of London and in the midst of my friends. But I am too old for new schemes, and especially such as would bridle my freedoms and liberalities."

This was Swift's way of saying that though some unknown patron had offered him a pleasant living in England, and it tempted him, he actually preferred Ireland, where he could be, as Dean, independent and liberal. He was closer to Ireland than he would admit. He did not during his stay in England even find time to go through the Oxford papers among which he had once thought he wanted to live over the days of his power, writing the history of the minister he had served and loved.

But if public affairs were disappointing, friendship and wit, for which Swift had his genius, were all he had looked forward to. His friends would not take his politics too seriously. " I hope," Bolingbroke wrote to " the three Yahoos of Twickenham, Jonathan, Alexander, John," " Jonathan's imagination of business will be succeeded by some imagination more becoming a professor of the divine science *la bagatelle*." During May and June Swift was as cheerful as he ever urged others to be. He was at Twickenham with Gay and Pope, content to let the world go its way if they could laugh at it. "Mr. Pope . . . prescribes all our visits without our knowledge, and Mr. Gay and I find ourselves often engaged for three or four days to come, and we neither of us dare dispute his pleasure." Bolingbroke and Bathurst were not far away. Congreve came out to dinner. Mrs. Howard had a house at Marble Hill. The Prince of Wales's court left London for Richmond where Swift made it his habit, as he put it, " to sponge a breakfast once a week."

The days were as busy, if not as weighty, as they had been for Swift when he spent them with the Ministry, but in the evenings he played backgammon with Pope's mother. Pope, Gay, and Swift went off for two weeks on horseback, to Lord Cobham's house at Stowe, to Bathurst's house at Cirencester, probably to Windsor Forest. Pope and Swift seem to have helped Gay with a ballad which he wrote at the inn at Wokingham. All three of them agreed upon a volume or volumes of miscellanies in which, as Pope described it, they were to " look like friends, side by side, serious and merry by turns, not in the stiff forms of learned authors, flattering each other and setting the rest of mankind at naught, but in a free, unimportant, natural easy manner, diverting others just as we diverted ourselves."

At the same time, Twickenham saw them working upon bigger schemes. Gay had his fables, taking from the behaviour of animals the rules for human conduct which he wittily versified for the little prince. Pope, angry at the spiteful dunces who had envied his success, was paying them off in a satire. Swift at first had thought they hardly deserved it. " Take care the bad poets do not outwit you, as they have served the good ones in every age, whom they have provoked to transmit their names to posterity." Swift himself almost never mentioned fools by name when he slaughtered them in prose or verse, unless the slaughter were political. But when he read Pope's satire he changed his mind, as Pope had now changed his. Pope was going to burn the verses. Swift saved them from the fire. When three such wits had come together they might as well all whip the world. Let Gay have his moral animals, and Pope his dunces. Swift would take mankind.

They read and discussed his Travels. Pope and Swift thought of means of publishing the book so stealthily that there would be no danger of prosecution. The printer, having seen a quarter of it, agreed to pay within six months the two hundred pounds which Pope made Swift demand. Only after Swift had left England the middle of August did the printer receive the manuscript, " he knew not whence, nor from whom, dropped at his house in the dark from a hackney coach " in which it is likely that the mystifying Pope enjoyed his subterfuge.

Secret enough, but not half as secret as Swift was about something dearer to him than any book. From the beginning of his visit he was worried about Stella,

who was very sick at home but tried to keep the news
from him. " I have these two months seen through
Mrs. Dingley's disguises," Swift wrote in July. Early
in that month he heard that Stella was in danger.
Though it destroyed his peace, he said nothing to his
friends in England. Bolingbroke knew that Swift had
a friend called Stella and gallantly assumed she was
his mistress. To Pope and Gay and Arbuthnot she was
at most only a vague shape in Ireland. Neither at
Twickenham nor at Whitehall, where Swift later lived
with Gay, was she more than that. Swift, so long used
to discretion where Stella was concerned, showed them
a wit's face, not a lover's heart. But his letters to his
friends in Ireland made plain how his grief had shaken
him.

" What you tell me of Mrs. Johnson I have long expected, with great oppression and heaviness of heart.
We have been perfect friends these thirty-five years.
Upon my advice they both came to Ireland and have
been ever since my constant companions ; and the
remainder of my life will be a very melancholy scene
when one of them is gone whom I most esteemed upon
the score of every good quality that can possibly
recommend a human creature. . . . My heart has
been so sunk that I have not been the same man, nor
ever shall be again, but drag on a wtetched life till it
shall please God to call me away. . . . I wish it could
be brought about that she might make her will. . . .

" Think how I am disposed while I write this, and
forgive the inconsistencies. I would not for the universe be present at such a trial of seeing her depart.

She will be among friends that upon her account and great worth will tend her with all possible care, where I should be a trouble to her and the greatest torment to myself. In case the matter should be desperate I would have you advise, if they come to town, that they should be lodged in some airy, healthy part and not in the deanery, which besides, you know, cannot but be a very improper thing for that house to breathe her last in. This I leave to your discretion, and I conjure you to burn this letter immediately, without telling the contents of it to any person alive.

" Pray write me every week, that I may know what steps to take ; for I am determined not to go to Ireland to find her just dead or dying. Nothing but extremity could make me familiar with those terrible words, applied to such a dear friend. Let her know I have bought her a repeating gold watch, for her ease in winter nights. I designed to have surprised her with it, but now I would have her know it, that she may see how my thoughts were always to make her easy. I am of opinion that there is not a greater folly than to con-tract too great and intimate a friendship, which must always leave the survivor miserable. . . . When you have read this letter twice, and retain what I desire, pray burn it and let all I have said lie only in your breast.

" Pray write every week. . . . I would rather have good news from you than Canterbury, though it were given me upon my own terms."

What other lover who ever lived could, staggering with grief and dread, have talked about the terms of his lover's will, measured her loss against the gain of an archbishopric, remembered that she must not die in his house, hesitated to go to her, and commanded that his anguish be kept secret ?

" One of the two oldest and dearest friends I have in the world is in so desperate a condition of health as makes me expect every post to hear of her death. It is the younger of the two with whom I have lived in the greatest friendship for thirty-three years. . . . For my part, as I value life very little, so the poor casual remains of it, after such a loss, would be a burden that I must heartily beg God Almighty to enable me to bear ; and I think there is not a greater folly than that of entering into too strict and particular a friendship, with the loss of which a man must be absolutely miserable, but especially at an age when it is too late to engage in a new friendship. Besides, this was a person of my own rearing and instructing, from childhood, who excelled in every good quality that can possibly accomplish a human creature. . . . Pardon me, I know not what I am saying. But believe me that violent friendship is much more lasting and as much engaging as violent love."

Towards the end of July, Swift, at Twickenham, was one day answering a letter from Sheridan. " The account you give me is nothing but what I have some time expected with the utmost agonies, and there is one aggravation of constraint, that where I am I am forced to put on an easy countenance. It was at this time the best office your friendship could do, not to deceive me. . . . I look upon this as the greatest event that can ever happen to me, but all my preparations will not suffice to make me bear it like a philosopher, nor altogether like a Christian. There hath been the most intimate friendship between us from her childhood, and the greatest merit, on her side, that ever was in one human creature towards another. Nay, if I were now near her I would not see her. I could not behave myself tolerably, and should redouble her sorrow. Judge in what a temper of mind I write this. The very time I am writing I conclude the fairest soul in the world hath left its body."

Just then Swift was interrupted. " Confusion ! that I am this moment called down to a visitor, when I am in the country and not in my power to deny myself."

He came back to his unfinished letter. " I have passed a very constrained hour, and now return to say I know not what. I have been long weary of the world, and shall for my small remainder of years be weary of life, having for ever lost that conversation which alone could make it tolerable. I fear while you are reading this you will be shedding tears at her funeral."

In a week Swift knew that, no matter what he faced, he must go to Ireland. Pope, ignorant of the full reason, was so unwilling to lose his friend that he travelled with him to Chester. " I felt the extreme heat of the weather," Pope said, " the inns, the roads, the confinement and closeness of the uneasy coach, and wished a hundred times I had either a deanery or a horse in my gift " to keep Swift in England or to make his journey more comfortable. But there were no words betwen them about Stella, as there were no words about her in any of the letters he wrote back to his English friends. Swift, so copious and eloquent about most of his passions, about this one was as quiet as a stone. Pope, who suspected something, risked only a hint in his wish that " you may find every friend you have there in the state you wish him or her." Talking about everything else in the world the two great wits rode in the uneasy coach to Chester, where Swift was prepared to find mortal news waiting for him. The only word from him about her is in a letter to an Irish friend two months later. " Mrs. Johnson is much recovered since I saw her first, but still very lean and low."

3

Pope wished " that your visits to us may have no other effect than the progress of a rich man to a remote estate, which he finds greater than he expected, which knowledge only serves to make him happier where he is, with no disagreeable prospect if ever he should choose to remove." And Swift, coming home from his rich estate in London, was received, Arbuthnot said, like a Lord-Lieutenant. When the ship was sighted in Dublin Bay the bells of the city were set to ringing. The Corporation, with less official citizens, went out in wherries to meet the " Dean, Drapier, Bickerstaff, or Gulliver." The docks had bunting, every street a bonfire. The populace cheered their defender as he landed and rode to his gloomy house.

If Swift was human, as well as Swift, he was warmed by this loud affection. But they were the people who had hooted him when he came over to be Dean, before he had fought for them about their copper farthings. " I have often reflected in how few hours, with a swift horse or a strong gale, a man may come among a people as unknown to him as the antipodes." Between Swift and the Irish, or between him and any body of men, it was too late for reconciliation. He had been an alien all his life, and he had proved it in his Travels. There the world would soon have a chance to study its disgusting face.

Travels into Several Remote Nations of the World, published 28th October, 1726, to vex the world rather than divert it, diverted it. Nobody spoke or apparently even thought of prosecution. " The politicians to a man agree," Pope and Gay wrote to Swift, " that it is free from particular reflections, but that the satire on general societies of men is too severe." Politicians were no more disposed than they were obliged to defend the human race against a libel. Mankind, invincibly abstract, invulnerably obtuse to general assaults, laughed. " From the highest to the lowest " the book was read, " from the cabinet council to the nursery." The Princess of Wales did not care, probably did not know, that she was supposed to have sat for the Queen of Brobdingnag. She was delighted. The Duchess of Marlborough was " in raptures " and willing to forgive her old enemy. Arbuthnot saw that the book was to be a classic, and forecast for it " as great a run as John Bunyan." The first impression was sold within a week. There were Dublin editions, and translations into French and Dutch within a year.

The third voyage, with its multiplied ridicule of pedants, pleased the least. That satire was too limited. Readers preferred to see all mankind in the refracting glass. Monkeys before a mirror, Swift might have said. They accepted the likenesses which they recognized, but they did not recognize those which might have vexed them. At least they did not take such likenesses to themselves. Untroubled by the satire, they enjoyed the story, so marvellous yet so circumstantial, so ingenious yet so simple. " Such a merry work," Arbuthnot called it. Who was there who could fail to be diverted by these adventures among pigmies and giants, on an island that moved through the air, in a land where horses used men as beasts ? Who minded that the traveller was a misanthrope ? Misanthropy did not hurt its objects, so long as it confined itself to words.

Swift, accusing mankind of every vice and folly, had thought of it as more sensitive or less frivolous than it was. He let drive with all his pitiless force, and the world applauded his witty marksmanship.

Stella having for the time recovered, Swift went again the next April to England, where the Earl of Peterborough thought the Dean ran the risk of becoming a bishop. The second visit was an anticlimax. Swift made no progress with the life of Oxford. He was completely out of favour with Walpole. Twickenham, happily as Pope welcomed Swift there, was not what it had seemed before. It was pleasant to talk with Pope about his dunces. It was pleasant to read the verses of the opera which Gay, to whom Swift had said that " a Newgate pastoral might make an odd, pretty sort of thing," was writing about rogues and beggars. It was pleasant to concoct their miscellanies, in which the poems to Stella were to appear. But it was unpleasant for Swift to be so deaf that he could hardly hear Pope's feeble voice or have a share in the conversation of the friends who came to see them. Swift began to feel that he was a burden. He would go to London.

He would go to France. Voltaire gave him letters of introduction. Swift exchanged opinions with his French translator, telling him, in his French, that if the Travels were calculated only for the British Isles then the traveller was a pitiable writer. The same vices and the same follies, he said, reigned everywhere, at least in all the civilized countries of Europe ; and the author who wrote only for one city, one province, one kingdom, or even one age so little deserved to be translated that he did not deserve to be read.

The death of George I and the accession to the throne of the Prince and Princess of Wales, who were the only royal friends Swift ever had, held him in England. Once more, and for the last time, he was disappointed. Walpole, after a fluttering interval, retained his power. Wit alone could not make a man a bishop.

Stella, it turned out, could not be well without Swift. He had left her settled in the deanery for the summer. In August Sheridan wrote that she was once more in danger. Swift, at the house of a kinsman in London, was helpless with his own malady.

" I walk like a drunken man, and am deafer than ever you knew me. If I had any tolerable health I would go this moment to Ireland. Yet I think I would not, considering the news I daily expect to hear from you. . . . I kept it [Sheridan's letter] an hour in my pocket with all the suspense of a man who expected to hear the worst news that fortune could give him, and at the same time was not able to hold up my head. . . . I know not whether it be an addition to my grief or not, that I am now extremely ill ; for it would have been a reproach to me to be in perfect health when such a friend is desperate. I do profess upon my salvation that the distressed and desperate condition of our friend makes life so indifferent to me, who by course of nature have so little left, that I do not think it worth the time to struggle. Yet I should think, according to what hath been formerly, that I may happen to overcome this present disorder. And to what advantage ? Why, to see the loss of that person for whose sake only life was worth preserving. . . . What have I to do in the world ? I never was in such agonies as when I received your letter and had it in my pocket. I am able to hold up my head no longer."

Still Swift would not tell his English friends about Stella. His secret had been buried in him too long to be dug up now. Too much of his heart would have come with it. Suddenly leaving London in September he lurched across England to Chester. Offered a passage from Parkgate in the official yacht, he refused, thinking he would be in Ireland sooner if he rode through Wales and shipped from Holyhead. There the winds delayed him for a week, spent in the smoky rooms of an inn which had no decent wine to drink, no books to read, no customers who could speak English.

Morning and afternoon he walked in the wind on the rocks. " I was so cunning these three last days that whenever I began to rage and storm at the weather I took special care to turn my face towards Ireland, in hopes by my breath to push the wind forward. But now I give up." Every night he dined alone, and had five dreary hours ahead of him before he went to bed. Sleep was no relief. He had fantastic dreams, such as that Bolingbroke was preaching in St. Patrick's and quoting Wycherley in his sermon. Morning was no restoration. Swift looked for the wind to change, and it would not change. " I live in suspense, which is the worst circumstance of human nature." There was nothing to do but " scribble or sit humdrum." He scribbled prose and verse.

> " *I never was in haste before*
> *To reach that slavish hateful shore.*
> *Before I always found the wind*
> *To me was most malicious kind.*
> *But now the danger of a friend*
> *On whom my fears and hopes depend,*
> *Absent from whom all climes are curst,*
> *With whom I'm happy in the worst,*
> *With rage impatient makes me wait*
> *A passage to the land I hate.*"

And when he finally got away the wind was so near a tempest that he was forced to land at Carlingford, sixty miles from Dublin, and complete his journey with " lazy dull horses."

This time Stella, though comforted by his return, was dying. Swift would not say so to Pope, to whom Sheridan had secretly written the truth. Again Pope hinted his sympathy. " To your bad health I fear there was added some disagreeable news from Ireland which might occasion your so sudden departure." Swift met the sympathy with a shield. His health, he said, had driven him home. " Here is my maintenance, and here my convenience." He invited Pope to Dublin. " I have a race of orderly elderly people of both sexes at command who are of no consequence and have gifts proper for attending us, who can bawl when I am deaf and tread softly when I am only giddy and would sleep." Six weeks later he repeated his invitation. " You may find about six rational, good, civil, learned, easy companions of the males ; fewer of the females, but many civil, hospitable, and ready to admire and adore."

Nothing about Stella, who had admired and adored beyond almost any woman who ever lived. Nothing about Stella to any man during the four months left to her. But Swift in October and November wrote three prayers which he used in her last sickness.

" Give her grace to continue sincerely thankful to Thee for the many favours Thou hast bestowed upon her : the ability and inclination and practice to do good, and those virtues which have procured the esteem and love of her friends and a most unspotted name in the world. . . . We beseech Thee likewise to compose her thoughts and preserve to her the use of her memory and reason during the course of her sickness. Give her a true conception of the vanity, folly, and insignificancy of all human things. . . . Let not our grief afflict her mind and thereby have an effect on her present distempers. Forgive the sorrow and weakness of those among us who sink under the grief and terror of losing so dear and useful a friend."

On a Sunday in January, when Swift had guests at his house, " about eight o'clock at night a servant brought me a note with an account of the death of the truest, most virtuous and valuable friend that I, or perhaps any other person, ever was blessed with. . . . As soon as I am left alone, which is about eleven at night, I resolve, for my own satisfaction, to say something of her life and character." He wrote of her parentage and girlhood, her intelligence and beauty (" only a little too fat "), her reasons for leaving England for Ireland. " Thus far I writ the same night between eleven and twelve."

The next day he wrote of her memory and judgment and gracefulness, " somewhat more than human," of her " civility, freedom, easiness, and sincerity." " All of us who had the happiness of her friendship agreed unanimously that in an afternoon or evening's conversation she never failed, before we parted, of delivering the best thing that was said in the company." He wrote of the love her servants felt for her. " My head aches, and I can write no more."

Tuesday was the day of the funeral at St. Patrick's. " My sickness will not suffer me to attend. It is now nine at night, and I am removed into another apartment that I may not see the light in the church, which is just over against the window of my bed-chamber." He wrote of her courage. She had once shot a burglar, trying to enter her house, and had killed him. She was never known to cry out with fear or weakness or affectation. He wrote of her manners, her reading in history, books of travel, the philosophers. " She had a true taste of wit and good sense, both in poetry and prose, and was a perfect good critic of style." He wrote of her fortune and her management of it.

Afterwards he wrote as he found time. He wrote of her charity, her tact, her modesty. " She rather chose men for her companions, the usual topic of ladies' discourse being such as she had little knowledge of, and less relish. Yet no man was upon the rack to entertain her, for she easily descended to anything that was innocent and diverting." She loved Ireland more than most natives, and detested " the tyranny and injustice of England in their treatment of this kingdom. She had indeed reason to love a country where she had the esteem and friendship of all who knew her, and the universal good report of all who ever heard of her."

This is as strange a language as love ever used, but it is a language of love, Swift's language, Swift's love. After he had written this he set down some of her sayings, which only a lover could have found as witty as Swift found them. After that he wrote not a word about her in any letter that survives. He is said never again to have spoken her name. He destroyed all her letters to him and all his letters to her except the journal which he had sent home from London. He would be as silent as Stella, the most silent of all famous lovers. But he could not quite equal her silence. On a paper containing some of her hair he wrote, it is said, the words " Only a woman's hair." A giant's sentimentality and a devil's contempt for it. Fire and ice.

VII

KING OF TRIFLERS

I

O N the day after Stella died the *Beggar's Opera* was first given in London, the Duke of Argyll starting the applause which in the end became a delighted clamour. Swift, who had been doubtful about the dramatic form which Gay had chosen, said the opera would do " more public service than all the ministers of state from Adam to Walpole." When it came to Dublin, and the Lord-Lieutenant approved of it, so did the Dean of St. Patrick's. Though Swift, who never went to the theatre, seems now to have made no exception, he spoke as from the Cathedral. Such humour would probably, he said with another moral comparison, " do more good than a thousand sermons of so stupid, so injudicious, and so prostitute a divine " as the court chaplain, later Archbishop of Canterbury, who had preached against the opera in London. Humour, Swift explained, was a " happy talent," " fixed to the very nature of man." Satire was public spirit "prompting men of genius and virtue to mend the world as far as they are able."

The defence of Gay became a defence of Swift. " I demand whether I have not as good a title to laugh as men have to be ridiculous, and to expose vice as another hath to be vicious. If I ridicule the follies and corruptions of a court, a ministry, or a senate, are they not amply paid by pensions, titles, and power, while I expect and desire no other reward than that of laughing with a few friends in a corner ? " Surely the objects of satire were as well off as the satirist. " If those who take offence think me in the wrong I am ready to change the scene with them whenever they please."

In March 1728 Swift impartially observed that " the *Beggar's Opera* has knocked down Gulliver ; I hope to see Pope's Dulness knock down the *Beggar's Opera.*" The *Dunciad* appeared in May. It was then without the inscription to Swift which, included the next year, made him feel " abstracted from everybody in the happiness of being recorded your friend while wit and humour and politeness shall have any memorial among us." But Swift had already seen the brilliant lines in which Pope named his friend with the greatest wits and complimented him with having driven Dulness out of Ireland, to settle, safe from him, in England.

> " *O thou ! whatever title please thine ear,*
> *Dean, Drapier, Bickerstaff, or Gulliver !*
> *Whether thou choose Cervantes' serious air,*
> *Or laugh and shake in Rabelais' easy chair,*
> *Or praise the Court, or magnify Mankind,*
> *Or thy grieved country's copper chains unbind ;*
> *From thy Bœotia though her power retires,*
> *Mourn not, my Swift, at aught our realm acquires.*
> *Here pleased behold her mighty wings outspread*
> *To hatch a new Saturnian age of lead.*"

Swift's Travels, Gay's Opera, Pope's Dunces : Twickenham had borne its satiric fruits. " Pope, Gay, and I," Swift later wrote, had done their best " to make folks merry and wise," acknowledging " no enemies except knaves and fools." But that episode had ended. Swift was never to see his friends again. Year after year they urged him to come back, and for a few years he often planned to go. Sickness and pride kept him in Ireland. The Court had no favours for him. Walpole was hopelessly in power. Bolingbroke, spinning out a slipshod philosophy for Pope to versify in his moral essays, tried to entice Swift to a living in Berkshire, half a day's journey from Uxbridge and Twickenham. Swift, relatively a rich man in Ireland, declined to become relatively a poor man in England. Letters would have to keep their friendship alive.

Half his life he lived in his letters to and from his English friends. Yet he wrote fitfully, fewer letters than he received. Much as he loved Arbuthnot, Swift was slow in writing to him. Gay might have to write twice or three times to draw an answer. When he could, Swift wrote to two of his friends at once : Bolingbroke and Pope, Arbuthnot and Pope, Pope and Gay, Gay and the Duchess of Queensberry, Gay's lively patron. " It is a very cold scent to continue a correspondence with one whom we never expect to see. . . . Mr. Pope and my Lord Bolingbroke themselves," Swift wrote in 1734, " begin to fail me."

The fellowship was mortal. Gay died in 1732. When the news came in a letter from Arbuthnot and Pope, Swift did not open it for five days, " by an impulse fore-

boding some misfortune." Arbuthnot died in 1735.
" The death of Mr. Gay and the Doctor," Swift wrote
to Pope, "have been terrible wounds near my heart.
Their living would have been a great comfort to me,
although I should never have seen them, like a sum of
money in a bank from which I should at least receive
annual interest, as I do from you and have done from
my Lord Bolingbroke." Bolingbroke after 1735 spent
most of his time in France. Only Pope and Swift were
left, Pope's mind to outlast Swift's, Swift's body to outlast Pope's.

There was no change in the affection which Swift
felt for his friends, but he could not help getting out of
touch with them. England was soon years away.
Despairing of English politics, in the interminable
hands of Walpole, Swift gave up his old concern for
government, except where Ireland was touched. He
saw London as the stage of a political melodrama, with
countless Whigs as the villain, and with no hero except
Pulteney and his Patriots. Swift ceased to follow, even
as much as he had done before, the turns and changes
of wit. London had Pope, and London had dunces.
In Ireland it was impossible to tell whom Pope was
slashing unless he spelled out the names of his victims.
When Swift read such writers, he was "out of all patience
to the present set of whifflers." England, London, the
Court might still be visible enough to Swift's memory,
but they no longer stirred with the life which had been
his passion and his magnet. They had stiffened to a
picture, and the years had set them in a frame.

It was time for Swift to learn, if he could learn, how
to live in Ireland without raging. For a year or so
after Stella's death he tried to learn. " Except absence
from friends," he wrote to Pope in May 1728, " I
confess freely that I have no discontent at living here,
beside what arises from a silly spirit of liberty, which as
it neither sours my drink nor hurts my meat nor spoils
my stomach farther than in imagination, so I resolve
to throw it off."

Sheridan, who of Swift's Irish friends had known
Stella best, plotted diversions. He took Swift south to
Wexford about Easter of that year. Together they
began in May to write the *Intelligencer*. This was meant
to be a weekly paper " to inform or divert or correct or
vex the town " of Dublin. The two contributors, who
had no editor to keep them going, did not lose interest
till after a dozen issues and did not stop till after
twenty. Sheridan got Swift invited in June to the house
of Sir Arthur Acheson at Market Hill near Armagh.
There from June to the next January, and during the
summers of 1729 and 1730, Swift lived with friends,
away from Dublin and the solitude of his deanery.

" I lived very easily in the country," he wrote to
Pope after the first visit. " Sir Arthur is a man of
sense, has a good voice, and my Lady a better. She is
perfectly well bred and desirous to improve her understanding, which is very good, but cultivated too much
like a fine lady. She was my pupil there, and severely
chid when she read wrong. With that, and walking

and making twenty little amusing improvements, and writing family verses of mirth by way of libels on my Lady, my time passed very well and in very good order."

Swift might have said more. Though his host was a member of the Irish Parliament and high sheriff of his county, and his wife was daughter of a man who had been for twenty years Chancellor of the Exchequer in Ireland, Swift with them was like an emperor on a friendly visit. They seem hardly to have questioned his imperial attitudes. The Dean might cut down one of the baronet's favourite trees or have his own way with such " little amusing improvements " as " zigzags and walks," " cradles and caves," " grottos and seats "—

> " *A hole where a rabbit*
> *Would scorn to inhabit,*
> *Dug out in an hour :*
> *He calls it a bower.*"

The Dean might tease the lady for her lack of flesh, calling her Skinnybonia, or for her lack of learning—

> " *He loves to be bitter at*
> *A lady illiterate.*"

The Dean might condemn her to " dull Bacon's Essays " or " poor Milton " while he, not at study or at prayer, amused himself with grooms and labourers. The Dean might insist that he, not the dairymaid, should shake cream in a bottle till, after three hours, there was butter for breakfast. The Dean might take it upon himself to build " two temples of magnific size "

213

for the " gentle goddess Cloacine." The Dean might come down to dinner when he chose, no matter who the guests. But he was still the Dean, the greatest man in Ireland, great politician, great wit. To say nothing of his company, his verses, spirited and various, were ten times a return for his entertainment. They would, Swift declared, make Market Hill as famous as Penshurst.

Swift was king enough in Ireland, if he wanted to be king. When he went back to Dublin in October 1729 after his second visit to Market Hill, he was received, a newspaper said, " with great joy by many of our principal citizens, who also on the same occasion caused the bells to ring in our cathedrals and had bonfires and other illuminations." Both candidates in an election then being held claimed the support of the Drapier, though it is not certain that either had it. One of them to win needed only to give out a letter which he said Swift had written to him. Early the next year the Dean, because he had been, as he now admitted, the Drapier, was given the freedom of the city in a gold box brought to him by the Lord Mayor and some of the aldermen. It was an honour usually reserved for " chief governors or persons in very high employment."

It was an honour, and Swift was gratified. Yet in a few weeks he was writing to Bolingbroke : " I ought to think that it is time for me to have done with the world, and so I would if I could get into a better before I was called into the best, and not die here in a rage, like a poisoned rat in a hole." His resolve to throw off his

214

discontent had not been kept. Such cheerfulness as he had felt at Market Hill had not survived his return to his solitary house. No sooner was he back than he wrote, or at least published, the most savage of all his pamphlets, the most terrible outcry of his misanthropy.

It was, he called it, a modest proposal. Everybody knew that Ireland was starving and nobody knew what to do about it. The problem was not so difficult. Put simply, it came to this : too little food, too many mouths. Swift had thought of a way to make more food and fewer mouths.

" I have been assured by a very knowing American of my acquaintance in London that a young healthy child well nursed is at a year old a most delicious, nourishing, and wholesome food, whether stewed, roasted, baked, or boiled, and I make no doubt that it will equally serve in a fricassee or a ragout." Of the children annually born in Ireland perhaps thirty thousand could be taken care of by their parents. Twenty thousand others might be kept " for breed, whereof only one fourth part to be males, which is more than we allow to sheep, black cattle, or swine." That would leave, he calculated, about a hundred thousand every year, " to be offered in sale to the persons of quality and fortune through the kingdom. . . . A child will make two dishes in an entertainment for friends, and when the family dines alone the fore or hind quarter will make a reasonable dish, and seasoned with a little pepper or salt will be very good boiled on the fourth day, especially in winter." Such food would be expensive, but within the reach of landlords, who,

" as they have already devoured most of the parents, seem to have the best title to the children."

One of his friends, Swift said, argued that in the present want of venison it might be well to supply it with boys and girls of twelve to fourteen. He himself could not agree. The boys of that age from much exercise would be thin and tough. The girls were too near the age when they might bear children themselves. " And besides, it is not improbable that some scrupulous people might be apt to censure such a practice (although indeed very unjustly) as a little bordering upon cruelty, which, I confess, hath always been with me the strongest objection against any project, however well intended." It would be enough to limit the proposal to children a year old. The older poor were already " dying and rotting, by cold and famine and filth and vermin, as fast as can be reasonably expected."

Plausibly, statistically, Swift went over the advantages and disadvantages of his scheme. The only real objection he could think of was that it would reduce the number of people in the kingdom. The best thing that could happen. It was Ireland he was writing about, not any other country " that ever was, is, or, I think, ever can be upon earth." Let no man talk of taxing absentees, or using Irish manufactures only, or going without luxuries, or forcing landlords to be generous and shopkeepers honest—as Swift himself had so long and often talked. None of those expedients had worked, or been tried. They were " vain, idle, visionary." This new proposal was " solid and real, of no expense and little trouble, full in our power." It would not even disoblige England. Ireland had hit upon a foodstuff which could not be exported because it could not stand much salt. Perhaps, however, " I could name a country which would be glad to eat up our whole nation without it."

Few of Swift's readers seem to have shuddered at his proposal. Lord Bathurst wrote from England that he had almost brought his wife round to the opinion that the youngest of their children should help provide for the eldest. After all, any sensible reader knew that the Irish children would not be eaten, at least in this forthright, economical way, just as he knew that there were no Houyhnhnms and no Yahoos. Swift, sensible readers said, was only joking, as the Irish bishop had said that Gulliver was only lying. Once more the misanthrope had run against mankind in the abstract.

For Swift there was nothing abstract about it. There was the actual disease. Here was the only sufficient cure. What if his flesh did creep when he recommended " buying the children alive, and dressing them hot from the knife " ? What if his nerves did rage when he advised that the mothers of the children " let them suck plentifully in the last month so as to render them plump and fat for a good table " ? So had his flesh crept and his nerves raged all over Ireland at the starved desert that England had made of it. If his cure violated the profoundest human instincts, so did the disease. Ask the parents if they would not have been better off if they had been sold for food at a year old instead of growing up to life in Ireland. Of course the proposal would not be carried out. Nothing so logical, nothing so mad and merciful, would ever be carried out. That was mankind. That was mankind.

Except for a few hints, a few urgings, a few arguments, a few accusations, all scattered and occasional, Swift after his modest proposal wrote no more prose about Ireland. "Looking upon this kingdom as absolutely desperate," he said in 1731, " I would not prescribe a dose to the dead."

3

All his life Swift had been alien, but he had never been so solitary as he now became. His misanthropy, however rooted in his constitution, however confirmed by his experience, however fortified by his blunt metaphysics, was not complete. He had had to be perverse to be so thorough. He had had to deny himself things that he wanted in order to round out his desolation. Even in his desolation, perverse but not altogether voluntary, he had needed habitual friends. He was not a man who could do without women. Stella, in his worst hours, had been friends and women. After her death he lacked what only a friend who was also a woman could give him. Without her to consider he settled into a dark preoccupation with himself. Without her to stir him to variety he sank into a tedious, disheartening, cold routine, hard and harder to break through.

At first he dined alone, or with his housekeeper, five nights out of seven. By 1736 he could say, with a grim flash, " nine days every week I dine at home."